NUMEROLOGY FOR BEGINNERS

Master and Design Your Perfect Life by Combining Numerology, Astrology, Numbers and Tarot to Unlock Your Destiny

By
Michelle Northrup

TABLE OF CONTENTS

INTRODUCTION

Numerology originated as a divination tool used primarily by pagans, but has since spread out and become a fascinating topic to many. Like people flock to their horoscopes to understand what they are destined for on a day to day basis, many people turn to numbers as a way to discover what is in store for that day for them.

As you begin to turn to numerology to discover your own destiny, you will quickly realize that numbers exist everywhere in our modern world. From our birth dates to our phone numbers and the way we count abundance through numerical values of finances, numbers are everywhere. When it comes to reading your own destiny through numbers, the numbers that you primarily want to pay attention to will pertain to your birth date and your name. Discovering how to find your numbers through some basic mathematical equations can help you learn more about who you are, uncover your natural tendencies, and find ways to enjoy this human experience even further. As with all predictive tools of this nature, numerology is a wonderful tool to help you understand how you can develop as a person, what patterns you can keep an eye out for, and what innate strengths you can tap into to help you discover your best self.

In this book, you are going to discover how numerology affects you, what you can learn about yourself based on your numbers, and how you can co-create the life of your dreams using numerology. By tapping into all of this knowledge, you are going to find yourself tapping directly into an entirely new realm of understanding yourself and understanding life around you. Be prepared to have your mind blown as you realize just how simple this all really is, while also understanding how insanely accurate it is as well.

To give you an idea of what you can expect, I have outlined some chapter summaries for you below.

In Part 1 with Chapters 1 through 5, you are going to discover the rich and diverse history of numerology and exactly how it impacts people. You are also going to discover how you can find your own numbers using these ancient understandings so that you can begin to get a feel for what your own chart looks like. With this guidance to create your very own chart, you are going to discover just how unique you are!

In Part 2 for Chapters 6 through 15 you are going to learn about what these numbers mean and how you can interpret them for your chart. This is going to help you get a clearer understanding for what your life and destiny paths are and what qualities you likely identify with based on your numbers. This is also going to help you determine more important information such as where your strengths and weaknesses lie and how you can improve your overall sense of wellbeing in life.

In Part 3 for Chapters 16 through 19 you are going to discover how numerology fits into other divination styles of readings, how you can use numerology in your everyday life, and how you can use numerology to improve your own intuitive senses. This is going to be a powerful opportunity for you to go from using numerology as a way to understand yourself more to using numerology as a tool to improve your overall life. This way, you truly do get the most out of your numerology experience.

I hope that in reading this book you find out just how incredible this divination tool is and how wonderful it can be to work with in your life. If you are ready to begin understanding and using numerology, then now is the time to get started. Be sure to take your time and enjoy the process, as there is plenty to learn and, naturally, you want the learning process to be filled with excitement! Please enjoy!

PART 1

Understanding Numbers

CHAPTER 1
Why Numbers Matter

Numbers matter for a variety of reasons. In our everyday lives, numbers are used to track things in many different ways. We use numbers to track the dollar value in our bank account, as the number on our bank cards, in our phone numbers and social security numbers, in our queue numbers when we stand in line, and in many other ways. We are virtually always counting something or being counted by something, which means that we are in contact with numbers every single day. Although many people may see this as just being a counting system, many others believe that these numbers hold a powerful value to them and that they are not chosen for us by chance but instead by destiny. Recognizing the value of numerology and using numerology in your daily life can help you understand many things about yourself and your life experiences which may support you in expanding your perception and experiencing a deeper sense of self-awareness.

What Is Numerology?
Numerology is known as being a divine connection between numbers and worldly events that we experience here on Earth. Numerology is known as an occult science that helps people determine what is going to happen on Earth based on the numbers relating to that situation, ranging from things such as health and relationships to careers and finances. Some people even believe that you can predict a miracle or a positive blessing based on the

alignment of these numbers, which makes receiving them considered to be a positive sign that allows you to feel confident that something good is coming your way.

Why Do People Use Numerology?

People have come to love numbers because they see them as a powerful way to connect with and communicate to the unseen. Whether you believe in God, the Universe, Source, a Higher Power, or an unknown greater presence that you prefer not to name, using numerology can be a great way to communicate back and forth with that entity. You can also use numerology to identify the energy associated with your life path, your life lessons, and your karmic destiny here on Earth. For many people, having access to this information feels like a powerful opportunity for them to begin making choices that are more aligned with their true purpose in life. For many more, the value of numerology is that they genuinely begin to feel as though they have a true purpose in life, which means that they can begin creating in alignment with this purpose. That way, they go from aimlessly wandering with deep feelings of despair and a lack of understanding to clearly walking toward everything that feels right for them.

One big reason why numerology is cherished and why many people adore this divination tool is because it is actually present in many different belief systems. Various religions and cultures have used numerology in one way or another as an opportunity to create significance through the value of numbers. Because of how flexible this divination tool is, many people with many different belief systems can use numerology as a tool to connect with the divine without feeling as though they are disobeying their religion. For example, Christians can use numerology because it is referenced in the Bible, whereas they cannot use tools like Tarot because these are considered to be witchcraft and are frowned upon by their religion.

Being able to have a divination tool that is so widely accepted by virtually every religious background out there means that many people can begin to understand themselves more deeply without feeling bad or wrong for what they are doing. This makes numerology not only a valuable tool but also a fascinating one because of how flexible it truly is and how accepted it is by many otherwise unaccepting belief systems. For those who are curious about divination and who want to use a divination tool without betraying their religion, numerology is a wonderful option.

Finally, numbers matter because they are believed to be the original format of the Universe. Virtually everything in the Universe can be broken down into a numerical value, hence why science and physics are such popular studies when it comes to understanding Earth and life itself. The fact that everything can be broken down into numbers and that numbers are used so widely means that numerology is not only one of the most commonly accepted tools, but it is also one of the most flexible tools in terms of what you can read with it. With numerology you can read everything from your own destiny to how compatible you are with other people or certain situations, and even what situations are right for you and which are not. You can also use numerology to increase your ability to communicate with the higher power that you believe in, or with the Universe itself. For this reason, numerology is understood to be a wildly powerful divination tool that everyone can benefit from learning about and using in their day to day lives. If you have been craving for something more or something deeper in your life, numerology can be a great opportunity for you to acquire that.

How Does Numerology Work?

When it comes to numerology, there are three numbers that are going to be most relevant to you as an individual. These three numbers include your psychic number, your destiny number, and your name number. Your psychic number represents how you perceive yourself, or through what lens you look at yourself. You will learn about how you tend to interact in your day to day life, what your character is like, and how your personality develops through your psychic number. You will learn more about your psychic number in Chapter 3.

Your destiny number helps you discover what it is that you came to Earth to learn, and what you are going to accomplish while you are here. Knowing your destiny number can help you discover your purpose in life while also giving you the opportunity to discover how you can fulfill your purpose. You are also going to learn about what your life lessons are based on your destiny number, which can help you become more aware of what it is that you may face in life and how you can face it with a deeper sense of awareness and preparedness.

Your name number helps you determine how you are going to develop relationships with other people, as well as how you will interact with other people in general. The name number is essentially your social number, which allows you to discover more about your social identity. Since your name can change over time, so too can your name number, which means that you can develop various elements of your identity through these changes.

Once you have discovered what these three numbers are for yourself, you will have your full chart developed. This way, you can begin using these numbers to understand more of yourself and develop an awareness around how you can proceed through life with a greater sense of alignment with yourself. For many people, having access to this knowledge feels like a guide for how they can proceed with decisions, life advancements, and important life changes, and you may find that it does just the same for you!

CHAPTER 2
The History Of Numerology

Numbers are known for having an inherent vibration, or an energy that each unique number possesses. According to people who study numerology, every number has its own vibration and we can read these vibrations to help us determine important information about people, places, things, and events. These vibrations can be likened to the vibration that new-age practitioners claim crystals, gemstones, colors, and essential oils have as well.

Numerology itself has a few different lines of history that help us identify where numerology comes from, and where different types of numerology comes from. The original line of numerology stems from Pythagoras, however additional numerology-like divination practices exist in other lines of history. We will explore a few of them below.

Pythagoras and The Original Numerology
While there are a few different beliefs surrounding where numerology came from, the most commonly accepted belief is that numerology stemmed from Pythagoras, a Greek philosopher who was born in Greece in about 569 B.C. Although we do not know much about Pythagoras or his work, there is still some information that remains from the work that he did that allows people to recognize what he contributed to the development of numerology. Some historians believe that Pythagoras himself was responsible

for possessing the information, but that the information we now see as a result of his work was actually put together by his followers.

Based on Pythagoras' teachings, numerology was considered to be a tool whereby you would discover numbers and then you would need to use your mind to apply a meaning to these numbers. Ideally, you would use your mind to investigate these relationships or meanings so that they would not simply pass by unnoticed. In other words, he believed in the importance of us giving relevance to these numbers, and he also believed that they were placed as divine guidance or tools for us to encounter and use in our journeys. This meant that the process of using numerology for divinity was a two-way street: the divine would place the numbers there for us, and we would place a meaning on the numbers. This is likely why some people will reject numerology as a divinity tool, too, as many people will want to rationalize the placement of the numbers as being mere coincidence as opposed to being something that was intentionally placed there for us. As a result, these individuals will likely reject the meaning of numerology and will instead choose to believe that the numbers are random and we are being overly sensitive for believing that they mean anything beyond the number at face value.

Christian Numerology Beliefs
In Christianity, traditional numerology is said to be a form of divination not unlike tarot or astrology, so traditional numerology is actually rejected by the faith. However, a variety of numerology

does exist in the sacred texts through sacred numbers and the "Jesus number" that have all remained intact throughout history. For that reason, although traditional numerology readings such as the ones we are looking into in this book may be rejected, the reality of sacred numbers, angel numbers, and the Jesus number all being accepted exists. This means that there is still a form of numerology that Christians can tap into that can help them use numerology in their lives without betraying their faith.

Modern Numerology

Modern numerology has actually evolved somewhat since Pythagoras' time. These days, as we have come to understand divination in an ever-evolving way, the modern reading styles are attributed to people like Ruth A. Drayer, Mrs. L. Dow Balliett, Juno Jordan, Florence Campbell, Lynn Buess, Mark Gruner, Faith Javane and Dusty Bunker, and Kathleen Roquemore. Each of these individuals has studied traditional numerology and developed their own studies based on what they came to understand which is typically where all modern numerology understandings and interpretations have stemmed from. If you are learning to use numerology in this day and age, chances are you are learning using a methodology that was adapted by one of these numerologists and so your study is a modification of the traditional reading method. Nonetheless, it can still be considered a traditional reading method as it is likely that your reading style has not evolved drastically from the original reading style. In this book, we are using a mixture of the modern understandings to ensure that we stay as close to the traditional reading style as possible.

CHAPTER 3
Your Psychic Number

Your psychic number, as mentioned above, is the number that helps you determine how you are going to perceive yourself based on numerology. This number reflects your perspective of your character, your personality, and ultimately who you are as a person. Having access to this number can help you develop an understanding around your core features and how you perceive the world around you so that you can get a deeper feeling for who you really are as a person.

How to Interpret Your Psychic Number

Your psychic number can be compared to your astrological sign: this is the number that says the most about who you are based on numerology. From this, you are going to learn valuable information about who you are and how you show up in the world. Knowing this number allows you to understand what your character is like, how you experience the world around you, and how people are most likely to see you from an external perspective.

When you discover your psychic number, you are likely going to feel a deep sense of connection to what that number means when you read about it in part 2. In part 2, you will discover how your psychic number actually impacts your personality, how you can recognize your strengths and weaknesses based on this number, and what you can do to balance yourself out using this number. Knowing this number will not only help you develop a deeper awareness around who you are, but it will also help you discover how you can approach different life experiences such as changes or decisions in a way that actually compliments your personality. For example, a person with a psychic number 1 and a person with a psychic number 6 are likely to approach life differently because 1 is the number of independence and 6 is the number of harmony and caregiving. A person with a number 1, then, would be more likely to make a decision based on themselves and their own needs whereas a person with a number 6 is more likely to make a decision based off of the people around them and their needs.

It is important that you aim to use this number not only to help you better understand yourself but also to help you better understand the core of who you are and how you can develop as a person. This deep understanding will help you understand how you can flow through life with greater ease and either co-create or manifest a life experience that is more likened to what you desire. Through this, you can stop trying to live your life based on other peoples' instruction which may not even be working for you and start living your life based on what actually works for you. In a sense, knowing this number can help you give yourself the permission that you need to become who you truly are and own your own approach to life.

How to Find Your Psychic Number
Your psychic number is based on your birth date, which is a number that cannot be altered in this lifetime. You get to your

psychic number by adding together your birth date until you either reach a single number, or a master number which is a repeating double-digit number (i.e. 11, 22, 33.)

An example of this equation would be:

Birth Date: 10th of June 1983

Numbers: (Day) 10

Equation: 1+0 = 1

Psychic Number: 1

CHAPTER 4
Your Name Number

Your name number reflects how you interact with other people, and how they interact with you. This number bears great significance in how you can connect with the people around you, so pay close attention to this number. Through it, not only can you develop an understanding around how your relationships will develop, but also around the patterns that you are likely going to carry throughout your relationships. Having a greater awareness around these natural tendencies can help you develop a deeper ability to connect with people in a healthier way and develop healthier relationships in general.

It is important to acknowledge that your name number can change based on your name changing throughout your lifetime, such as if you get married and start going by a different name. Recognizing this helps you become aware of the fact that how you interact with people can change, too, so that you can transition your awareness anytime your name changes.

How to Interpret Your Name Number
Your name number is going to be an important number in regards to how you relate to other people. This is going to give you a stronger understanding around relationship-based information such as how you relate to other people, the roles that you give them in your life, and the life cycles that your relationships tend to

operate by. When you know your name number, you can begin to understand why you behave the way you do in relationships, how you contribute to relationships, and what strengths and weaknesses you tend to carry in your relationships. This can tell you everything from why you tend to shut down or close off in relationships or why you are "clingy" and find yourself attaching closely to the people in your life. Any quirks or tendencies that you have in your relationships will all be predicted by the name number.

You are also going to understand why you attract the people you attract into your life, and how people tend to treat and view you in relationships. This is going to help you have a stronger understanding around why people behave certain ways toward you, what positive and negative attributes you tend to receive in relationships, and why certain characteristics may frequently be present in your relationships. In this aspect, we are talking about characteristics that may not be entirely your fault, such as people regularly doing nice things for you, seemingly out of nowhere, or betraying you despite them generally being fairly decent people. The more you can understand your numerology and how it contributes to your relationships, the easier it will be for you to have an awareness around these relationship tendencies so that you can overcome these unwanted patterns.

How to Find Your Name Number

You find your name number by using a numerology chart and locating the respective number for each letter in your name, and then adding them all together until they reach a certain numerological value. The different types of numerology have different types of name charts, but the most commonly accepted, standard, and traditional name chart is read using a simple system. You can find that chart below:

#	Letters
1	A, J, S
2	B, K, T
3	C, L, U
4	D, M, V
5	E, N, W
6	F, O, X
7	G, P, Y
8	H, Q, Z
9	I, R

So, if your name was "Samantha Louise Smith" your name would be calculated as follows:

Name: Samantha Louise Smith

Numerical Values: S=1, A=1, M=4, A=1, N=4, T=2, H=8, A=1, L=3, O=6, U=3, I=9, S=1, E=5, S=1, M=4, I=9, T=2, H=8.

Equation:

1+1+4+1+4+2+8+1+3+6+3+9+1+5+1+4+9+2+8 = 73, 7+3 = 1

Name Number: 1

CHAPTER 5
Your Destiny Number

Your destiny number is calculated by your birthday, and it is responsible for helping you determine what you are going to experience in this lifetime. When people begin using numerology, their destiny number is often the first number that they discover as it is the most popular number to talk about in numerology. As you can expect, your destiny number cannot be changed since you cannot change the day that you were born. So, your destiny number remains with you for your entire journey. The destiny number is sometimes called your life path number too, as it helps you determine what your life path is likely to be in this lifetime, offering you great information around what you are likely to encounter and how.

How to Interpret Your Destiny Number
Your destiny number is going to tell you everything from what your life purpose is to what karmic patterns you are likely going to encounter in your lifetime. Your destiny number will help you discover who is likely to come across your path, what lessons you are going to learn, what patterns you are going to see repeating throughout your life, and what challenges you are likely to face. When you identify your destiny number, you may begin to feel rather shocked to realize that your life so far has resonated very well with this particular number. You may even begin to feel a sense of peace in realizing that many of the challenges and

struggles that you have faced in your life were predetermined and that this is nothing unusual for you. Realizing that what you are going through in life is exactly what you were meant to go through can be a breath of fresh air for many as they come to understand the fact that it being placed in your life means that you were meant to go through it. Thus, if you were meant to go through it, you were also meant to have or develop the strength to help you get through it rather than feeling like there is no hope and you are at its mercy for the rest of your life.

In addition to helping you understand and come to peace with your life challenges and struggles, knowing your destiny number can also help you understand and come to peace with your purpose in life. Many people who do not yet know their destiny number may not yet fully understand what their purpose is in life. For that reason, they may be aimlessly wandering around trying to discover exactly what it is that they are meant to be doing with their lives. Or, they may find that they are clear on what they are meant to be doing but that they are not sure as to why. Having your destiny number can help you answer these important questions about yourself, thus allowing you to have an even deeper understanding around why you are here and what you are meant to accomplish while you are here.

How to Find Your Destiny Number
Finding your destiny number comes from turning your entire birthday into an equation. It starts by identifying the numerical

values of your birthday and then adding them together until you get one whole, single digit number. That is, unless your equation brings you to a master number such as 11, 22, 33, or otherwise in which case you leave it as is since these numbers have their own special meaning as well.

Here is an example of the destiny number equation:

Birthday: August 16, 2010

Numerical Value: 08/16/2010

Equation: 0+8+1+6+2+0+1+0 = 18, 1+8 = 9

Destiny Number: 9

PART 2
The Meanings Of The Personality Numbers

CHAPTER 6
Number 1: The Independent One

If you have the number one in your chart, you have the energy of independence flowing deep in your numerology chart. Number ones are known for being the first number, therefore they resonate deeply with new beginnings and fresh starts, too. In addition to fresh starts and independence, number ones love to be leaders.

Number One Vibration
Number one is known for having a masculine vibration, as it thrives on self-reliance, strength, forcefulness, and independence. Number one loves new beginnings, creating new things, and being unique and different from everything around it. This energy is very positive and craves power, as well as powerful raw energy and assertiveness. The number one vibration is highly instinctive and intuitive and is known for initiating new things in the world through these two energies. Number one energy in your chart symbolizes you being very open to trying new things, pioneering a new way to do things, and leading the way through these fresh starts. Chances are, you came up with the idea or perfected it from someone else and now you want to lead everyone down the path of creating this new idea in reality.

One as A Psychic Number

As a psychic number, one energy symbolizes a person who wants to be in the leadership position. Number ones love being the boss, taking control, and leading teams of people to success in various ventures. They are very inventive and will likely want to find the optimal way to do things and then instruct and guide everyone else to do it this way, too, so that everyone can perform to their high standards. They want to know that they are the best at everything they are doing, and they will judge themselves based on the strengths and qualities of any teams they lead, so those who take on careers that involve leadership will be very hard on their team. That being said, they will generally be polite when they are guiding their team to success, although they may not necessarily possess *true* compassion. In other words, you may have a tendency to fake compassion so that the individual you are leading feels like they have experienced compassion, therefore they are more likely to get back to performing at a higher standard. For this reason, the number one's compassion when it comes to projects is not always genuine but will often come with an underhanded meaning. When the number one is showing true compassion though you best believe that they are showing the best compassion possible. They will be likely to take care to listen effectively, hear your needs, and respond in the best way possible because they want to be the best compassionate person there is, based on their nature of always wanting to be the best.

As a number one, you likely find that you are a very assertive and bossy person in general. You may regularly hear feedback about how bossy you are or about how you tend to want things to be "your way." To you, your way is the best way which is why you instinctively assume that everyone else wants to behave this way, too. You are likely surprised to learn that people have different preferences and that they may wish to do things in other ways, particularly when you see these other ways as being inferior. It may take you some time to learn that there are many ways to accomplish the same goal and that it is perfectly okay for other people to do things differently from how you do them.

When it comes to how you carry yourself in life, you are likely known for being very particular and organized. You like things done a certain way because this brings you happiness and fulfillment. You not only want things to be done a certain way so that they are done right in your eyes, but also because you feel this brings you recognition for what you have done which gives you a big boost of pride. You are a very proud person, which can sometimes either become or can be mistaken as becoming egoic or self-centered. You love to be acknowledged for what you do and, in many cases, you will seek out praise by over performing and overachieving and then asking questions in a way that welcomes praise from the people around you. You may find that at times you become a people-pleaser or a perfectionist because of your constant need to be the very best and receive praise from others.

One as A Name Number

If you have a number one in the position of your name number on your chart, then the way that you lead in relationships is very masculine and leadership-oriented. You like to be the leader in relationships, typically wanting things done your way so that you can feel safe and secure. When someone else tries to take over the role of being a leader you may feel uncomfortable and find that you clash with these individuals, which can either lead to relationships filled with toxic arguments, or you being very passive as you "check out" of the relationships that you are in. To you, a relationship where you are not accepted as the leader is a relationship where you feel unappreciated and unreceived, and so it is hard for you to contribute. When someone else does not accept you leading or laying the groundwork for the relationship, you may feel deeply rejected by that person, and that can hurt big time.

You like to make people happy, partially because you love other people being happy in general and partially because you like how it looks on you when you have positive relationships. When the people in your life have nothing but good things to say about you, it reflects positively on you and leaves you feeling very good about yourself and what you contribute to the world around you. Also, you like to be the one who suggests things such as taking relationships to the next level or doing something significant together so that you can take responsibility for that achievement in your relationship. This way, when you announce your news to other people you can have your pride boosted by knowing that all of the praise is ultimately coming toward you for you being the one to initiate this new change in your relationship. Again, you have a tendency to be very underhanded in your relationships because at the end of the day you are motivated by your own reputation and what people think of you. This does not necessarily mean that you are a bad person or that you are selfish in relationships, but it does mean that you are at risk for developing this approach in relationships. If you remain unaware of this pattern, you may find that you drive people away from your self-centeredness as they begin to recognize that you are only in the relationship for your own self-validation. Becoming aware of this pattern allows you to recognize your motivation of having a positive reputation so that you can use this to encourage you to continue contributing while also consciously choosing to become more mindful about engaging in selfless acts of love and compassion.

Despite the fact that it can sometimes feel like everything needs to revolve around you, you are passionate about love. Love brings you happiness and makes you feel good, and it also tends to inspire you to have the energy to spark your new beginnings in life. You likely find that you are the type of person who either has deep and close connections with people, or no connections at all. You do not like partial relationships where you are sort of close with people as these can feel very ingenuine to you. Again, you like the best of the best, including the best quality of relationships.

One as A Destiny Number

When it comes to your destiny number, a number one can signify this being a lifetime of many new things. Many numerologists believe that a number one destiny number signifies you being in your first incarnation on Earth, so you may be what some consider a "young soul" or a soul that has yet to experience the spiritual maturity of many lifetimes. Since you are new to this Earth, numerologists say that virtually everything you are going to experience is going to be new to you, so truly this is a lifetime of exposing yourself to as many new things as possible.

On the positive side of being a number one destiny number, you are coming here very open-minded and with plenty to learn. Because you have no information lingering on a soul level, you are unlikely to be jaded toward any particular thing which means you are unlikely to have deep-rooted fears from past life experiences. For example, it is unlikely that you have an intense fear of fire stemming from being burned in a past life, because according to numerologists you have never had a past life. For this reason, you are likely to be less inhibited than other life path numbers which means that you are more likely to have the confidence and bravery needed to actually try out all of these new things. This can bring a deep sense of confidence, self-esteem, and self-worth.

The negative side of being so open and confident is that you have also not had many opportunities to experience and overcome feelings of pain, so painful experiences are more likely to strike deep for you. You are likely going to find that anything from rejection to heartbreak feels far worse to you because you have not yet learned how to process the energy of these deeply painful emotions. Because of how intense these emotions can be, you may find that you have the opportunity for many traumas to root deeply within you in this lifetime which can lead to you taking these traumas forward with you if you do not heal them. Being very intentional about healing your traumatic experiences in this lifetime can help prevent you from bringing any of these experiences forward as deep-rooted fears in future lifetimes.

One big benefit of being a number one destiny path is that you likely do not carry much karma with you in this lifetime. Any karma that you are carrying on Earth will have been accumulated in this lifetime, meaning that you can do the work of neutralizing this karma in this lifetime so that you do not carry as much forward with you. If you have been self-centered to the point of toxicity in your life so far, you may find that you have accumulated a lot of karma in your lifetime. This can be one of the negative side effects of being a number one destiny path: you do not yet understand karma so your excessive self-centered can sometimes lead to you being cruel or harmful to those around you. As a result, you may accumulate karma quickly if you are not taking the time to become aware of this potential pattern and work toward balancing it as you go. If you have already accumulated a lot of karma, do not fret, you can still do the work of releasing this karma in this lifetime so that you do not carry it all forward with you into future lifetimes. Your self-awareness is a massive asset to you at this time.

CHAPTER 7
Number 2: The Cooperative Peacemaker

The number two energy is classified as the cooperative peacemaker because number two individuals are those who value peace. A number two in your chart means that you really appreciate having peace and comfort in your life and you will often go to great lengths to bring these qualities into your life. To you, peace is likely going to be a very important element in at least one area of your life, and you will likely deny any experiences that do not lend to your peace. Let's look deeper into some more qualities associated with the number two in numerology.

Number Two Vibration
The number two vibrates at a very feminine energy, as it is receptive and cooperative. The number two wants peace and harmony in life and uses its cooperation and receptivity to welcome these two qualities in, which allows them to experience it with ease, so long as no one takes advantage of their receptivity and cooperation. A number two energy also vibrates with qualities like: gentleness, kindness, justice, selflessness, intuition, poise, flexibility, and grace. If you are vibrating with the number two energy, you are vibrating with an energy that is very harmonious and peaceful in every way.

Two as A Psychic Number

Individuals who have the number two in their psychic number position are very peaceful individuals. They may be regarded as quiet and cooperative because they do not enjoy confrontation. A number two psychic position is also known for being considerate and friendly, as well as favoring positions of service and duty. Number two people have a character that is very soft and gentle, and often find themselves being very flexible and sensitive in their lives. To them, these two qualities support them in remaining peaceful in their experiences.

When an individual with a psychic number two is vibrating in a positive two energy they are compassionate and harmonious without losing their own voice. They know how to communicate effectively and they are excellent at getting what they need without causing too many ripples to make it happen. In the face of conflict, a two person can keep things calm by deescalating the energy and infusing it with peace. Oftentimes, people who attempt to argue with a number two psychic person will find themselves quickly calming down from intense emotions so that they can communicate in a more reasonable and polite manner. This two energy will likely find themselves regularly leaning toward optimism and positivity and will always want to look for the silver lining in life as this is where the joy and peace exists. They like to find ways to express themselves in a quiet and calm manner, and may sometimes appear to come across as delicate or very feminine as a result of this preference. Do not be surprised, though, when a two energy does get confrontational. If they truly feel that their peace is being disturbed and that the situation or person disturbing their peace is not backing down, a two will stand up and fight for themselves. That being said, they are hard to stir and will often settle back down quickly after a moment of frustration because they truly do not like to live in this energy.

A two who is living in a negative shadow aspect of two energy is someone who may find themselves refusing to speak their truth or own their experiences for fear of being confronted by other people. They may minimize their own opinions or truths as a way to avoid causing disruption in their lives so that they do not draw negative attention to themselves. This can lead to a two energy feeling unheard and disrespected because, to them, everyone deserves to be met with the same compassion and peace in life and they feel rejected when they are not met with this by others. Unfortunately, the two will rarely realize that it is their own people pleasing skills that has taught the people in their lives to ignore their opinion or overlook what they have to say. In addition to staying quiet when they ought to speak up, a two energy may become so cooperative for others that they are taken advantage of. In careers or relationships, they are at risk of being dealt more than they can reasonably handle because they do not want to say no and cause frustration or disappointment for other people. As well, they may find themselves excessively sucking up to people who have a tendency to be overly dramatic or cruel because they want to try and balance the situation they are in. Twos in a negative aspect can be known to try and single-handedly manage the emotions of every situation as a way to try and keep control over the peace. This can lead to unnecessary burdens and deep feelings of pain and rejection when situations inevitably fall apart and they hold themselves responsible for it.

Two as A Name Number

If you have a two in your name number position, you are a person who values peace and cooperation in your relationships. You love being in relationships with people who work together with you to experience a peaceful and fun life as this allows you to feel calm and relaxed. You are perfectly happy doing calm things like walking around a quiet park and feeding the ducks or sitting on your patio enjoying an iced tea because these are the things that keep you relatively settled. Depending on the other numbers in your chart, you may find peace in being more adventurous or outgoing or you may find peace in being more quiet and introverted. Either way, once you have your definition of peace you are going to seek out and attract people who have a similar preference towards peace in their own lives as well. If you are clear on what peace looks and feels like for you, attracting people who are also lowkey and laid back in the same ways as you will be easy.

When you are in flow with your number two name number in relationships, you find that your relationships are very calm and easy going. You likely do not argue with people often, and you do not hold space for people who regularly want to argue with you. If someone does become overly argumentative or otherwise regularly disturbs your peace you will quickly uphold your boundaries and release the relationship to avoid having this drama in your space. For those who favor calmness such as yourself, your relationship will be what some consider to be dreamy. You often find that you both contribute to the relationship with a deep level of respect and that you both value each other's happiness. You love to get together and enjoy positive support and encouragement, so it is common for you to be the cheerleader of your social circle. You also appreciate receiving encouragement back and may even seek it from time to time, as this feels like positive validation to you. Another positive aspect of you in relationships is that you are very faithful and trustworthy and you often seek out friends and partners who are as well, so there is rarely any reason for you or your partners to worry about betrayal.

If you are out of flow with your number two name number, you may find that your relationships feel very taxing and draining. Because of how cooperative you are, you may be manipulated into becoming attached in relationships that are toxic to you. People who are manipulative may recognize that you are cooperative and may take advantage of you to fulfill their own needs, rarely having any consideration toward you and your needs. Avoiding self-centered people who do not respect boundaries will be necessary so that you are not manipulated for your cooperative tendencies. You also need to be cautious about your tendency of quieting yourself down to avoid confrontation, or minimizing your personality to avoid rejection. Owning who you are and being true to yourself and your opinion is necessary for you to avoid being drained in relationships by constantly having to put on a mask that is not true to who you really are.

Two as A Destiny Number

If you have two as a destiny number, you likely identify with words like empath and lightworker, and these tie in closely to what your life purpose is. As your destiny number, a number two energy suggests that you are passionate about promoting world peace and that you are likely to engage in your life in ways that promotes peace in general. You likely root for the underdog, are big into justice, and find yourself wanting to support those around you. You may be drawn to career paths like being a social worker, a volunteer person, being a lawyer, or being a therapist. You want to help people increase the peace in their lives either by fighting for them or by giving them the tools that they need to seek peace and bring it in.

You may face some very difficult lessons in life as you realize that not everyone is as committed to peace as you are, which can lead to deep-rooted feelings of discomfort and despair. You may find yourself feeling depressed or overwhelmed when you consider the present state of the world as you realize that we still deal with a lot of cruelty and injustice, which to you simply makes no sense. In your eyes, it is common sense that everyone deserves equality and that we should respect all people and living things in the same way. In fact, you may even find that you are fighting not only for the peace and wellbeing of fellow humans but also for animals as you advocate for their wellbeing, too. You may even favor a vegetarian or vegan diet to show your support as the idea of cruelty to animals through eating an animal-based diet may be too much for you to handle.

A big lesson for you will be learning how to preserve your inner peace while respecting the world around you. You will be presented with many lessons and karmic patterns that help you identify how you can live in peace with those around you. You are going to be learning about how you can have an opinion while also honoring the opinions of others, how you can engage in relationships that include respect being given and received, and how you can protect yourself against people who lack peace without disturbing your own peace. Boundaries and a willingness to see yourself as independent of other people is a big one here as you are learning how to engage in the collective without taking the responsibility of the world onto your own shoulders.

According to numerologists, a number two life path suggests that you are still early on in your spiritual maturity so you are not yet considered an old soul. For this reason, you may still struggle to fully understand Earth and the experiences that you are having here on Earth from a spiritual and energetic perspective. On one hand you have a very innocent and pure belief system that comes with not truly knowing, much like a child who has yet to witness how the world truly works. On the other hand, you have been here before so you may possess a degree of arrogance that has you feeling like you know more than you actually understand. Beware of this so that you can keep yourself in check and focus on consciously staying open to the lessons that you have yet to learn here on Earth.

CHAPTER 8
Number 3: The Self-Expression And Creative

The number three is sometimes referred to as the socialite number because this is a number that thrives in social environments. Number threes tend to be extroverted and find themselves vibrating at a very energetic and outgoing level. If you have a number three in your chart, chances are you are eccentric and outgoing and this is a fundamental part of who you are. Read on to find out what other attributes resonate with the number three energy!

Number Three Vibration
The energy of the number three is very harmonious, but in a far more outgoing way than the number two. Whereas number two values peace, number three values creativity and self-expression. A number three can be likened to an eccentric and sophisticated art major at an artists' event, enjoying drinks and being identified as the life of the party. This individual loves to get around and meet people because that is how they find inspiration, and they use that inspiration to get creative so that they can either create something new or create a new element of their self-expression. This number is very balanced, outgoing, and humorous. They are also known for being imaginative and intelligent since they spend so much of their time curiously exploring and experiencing the world around them so that they can feed their ever-wandering mind.

Three as A Psychic Number

If you have three as a psychic number, you are likely known for being loud and eccentric. Your friends and family may even describe you as weird, unique, out there, or alternative. Living a normal life sounds boring to you as it does not leave you with much room for creativity and self-expression, so you are likely drawn to living life in your own unique way. How this looks, exactly, will depend on who you are and what other attributes you have in your chart. One expression of this may be that you are very driven and so you use your creativity and self-expression to launch your own business venture and carve out your own path in life. You may be so opposed to traditional living that you truly do everything you can to be your own individual. The word "hipster" may be a reasonable word to describe who you are and how you show up for life. Another potential expression is that you do follow a traditional life path, but you liven it up with your own unique signature touch. This signature touch could be anything from how you speak and how you share your humor to how you dress yourself for the day.

You are known for having good taste and are likely responsible for introducing your friends to the latest trends in pop culture and life in general because you always seem to be at the forefront of it all. Your curious mind keeps you looking into everything that reflects your personal self-expression preferences, so you are always finding new ideas that you are willing to try out. Sometimes these ideas may be horrible, like tie-dye overalls, but still you manage to pull them off somehow. You are known for making the impossible

possible because you can creatively find your way to a solution in virtually any situation in your life.

It is likely that you are also known for your great sense of humor, too, as you have a tendency to love laughter and you enjoy it even more when you can make others laugh with you. Do not mistake this for people pleasing though: you will say a joke because you know it will make you laugh, other people laughing with you is just a happy bonus.

You may find that you possess a very youthful and sometimes even childish vibe because you are so outgoing. As well, you are known for being intuitive or possibly even tapped into psychic abilities because you are so creative and tapped into your imagination. It is likely that manifesting comes easy to you and that you were surprised when you learned that it does not come easy for everyone else because to you it is just a natural part of life. You are so in tune with your mind that making things happen through thought power is easy for you.

Three as A Name Number

If you have a number three as a name number, you likely have a very active and highly engaged social life. Number threes are known for thriving on a high amount of social interaction, so whether you are going out with friends every night of the week or simply getting out of the house and interacting with the barista for a few extra minutes on your way to work, you are always socializing. Your phone is likely filled with numbers, or at least your social media is buzzing. Chances are you do not mind phone calls nearly as much as other people seem to because you love a good opportunity to catch up with the people you care about so that you can chat for hours on end. If you are not a big phone call person, you are likely still engaging in multiple text chats or instant messaging chats at once so that you can keep your mind stimulated.

When you are in positive flow with your number three name number, you are an excellent friend to have. You likely attract very high energy people into your life who are known for being just as outgoing as you are, and your group likely gets into all sorts of crazy experiences. You may even find yourself comparing your group to those that you see on TV where you are constantly getting into all sorts of unique and exciting experiences. A simple night out at a café can become a crazy autobiography-worthy experience with you because of the energy that you naturally attract into your life. The people in your life either need to be as high energy as you are or they need to appreciate your high energy in order to stick around, otherwise they are not going to last long. You likely find that your relationships are very positive, although they may also be complex at times.

In a negative flow, you can come across as loud and overwhelming. This happens when you are not attracting the right people into your life so you find yourself engaging in friendships with people who do not receive your outgoing personality well. If you are surrounding yourself with people who do not match or appreciate your energy you may begin to turn that high energy into a sabotaging energy. Rather than getting the energy out and enjoying fun and highly engaged relationships you may instead find yourself arguing with the people around you or even doubting yourself and bullying yourself for being bad or wrong for your naturally outgoing personality. If you are really out of tune with yourself you may even become destructive or manipulative in your relationships as you try to change people into being more outgoing and high energy like you are. When you realize it does not work you may try harder to pressure them into changing, rather than accepting that they are not as outgoing as you are and finding friends or partners who are. This can lead to a negative spiral of self-sabotaging and then toxic relationships that do not meet your needs as you never learn to validate yourself or give yourself permission to be the loud version of you that you have been hiding.

Three as A Destiny Number
If you have three as a destiny number, you have a very broad spectrum of things that you could do in your life. Your intense creativity means that you can truly create anything that you want, so it is likely that you are going to be drawn to life purposes or paths that nurture your creativity and self-expression. Threes are known for being the inventor or the entrepreneurs of the world because of just how creative they are. Unlike a one energy who will create for the purpose of having solutions so that they can be the best, threes create for the purpose of creating and expressing themselves which means that they are not afraid of looking silly. As a result of this, a

three energy will happily create new things and try new ventures all the time and will not let failed creations or unwanted outcomes prevent them from carrying on. They will continue to create and work toward sharing their creations with the world regardless of how many times they have failed at this venture. Common career paths for creative number threes include intuitive paths such as being psychics or life coaches, artists, musicians, fashion-related careers, and anything else that allows them to creatively express themselves.

Life challenges faced by the number three often fall back toward them being loud and outgoing with their energies. Because of how big their energy can be, a number three who does not know how to validate themselves and surround themselves by equally outgoing or accepting people can begin to feel like they have to minimize themselves which leads to destruction, either of self or of others. A person with a three-destiny path is going to need to learn how to validate themselves and surround themselves with people who appreciate and accept their creativity and who are okay with their louder voices and higher energies. They are also going to need to learn how to quietly and respectfully walk away from anyone who is not okay with who they are, as the loud falling out will only lead to them feeling silly and rejected in the end.

Another big life lesson is learning that not everything goes their way. Despite wanting to be a free-flowing and adventurous individual, the world itself does have a structure that it flows with and, to a degree, learning how to flow with the world as it is will be an extremely important life lesson. Threes have a tendency to question why we need to have jobs at all, or why the cost of living has to be so high particularly when it cuts into them being able to follow their chosen life path. Finding a way to conform to society without losing their personal sense of freedom and authenticity will be a big lesson, and they will benefit greatly from learning how to fit in without losing a sense of who they are. The more that they can balance modern living with being alternative or different, the better a three is going to feel in the long run.

CHAPTER 9
Number 4: The Devoted Worker

The number four energy is known for being one that revolves around work and progress. Number fours are practical, organized, and highly devoted. They are known for their hard-working tendencies and their desire to acquire many achievements in their lifetime. They are driven by their need to achieve more and progress with things in their life. Let's dig deeper into other attributes of the number four energy.

Number Four Vibration
On a vibrational level, a number four is a masculine energy as it wants to work and push forward to put things in order. Despite being a masculine energy, the number four is not typically a loud energy but more of a persistent energy that likes to see things getting done. They are the ones who will keep going until the job is done, rather than clock out early, because they love knowing that they have achieved something. While they love recognition and validation, a four energy will complete the job regardless of what praise they are getting because the inner sense of accomplishment is plenty enough. Words that tend to resonate with the number four energy include: devotion, constructiveness, practicality, determination, production, traditional, honesty, and pragmatic.

Four as A Psychic Number

As a psychic number, the number four energy shows up in individuals who can sometimes be recognized as workaholics. They tend to value their work and progress more than anything else in the world, and if they cannot see how something can be turned into a goal that can be achieved, they have a hard time developing the drive to stay committed to it. They are known for turning everything into a project and, once they have, they will show up with their fully committed energy and they will push through virtually anything to get the results that they want.

A number four psychic number is the type of person who will set goals at variously timed lengths so that they always have something to work toward and they can always experience a sense of achievement. The more that a four feels that they are achieving their desires, the more a four is going to feel at peace in their life. Shorter goals like daily and weekly goals are necessary for a number four to feel like they are on the right path, but at the end of the day they are mostly focused on their larger goals that have the biggest meaning to them. Their goals exist in all areas of their life, and they are often very clearly focused on what they want and how they want their lives to look. Because of how committed they are to their long-term goals, fours are often willing to be flexible in their shorter term goals because they know that flexibility here will lead to their successful acquisition of their larger goals. Despite their flexibility in their short-term goals, the four rarely has any level of flexibility in their long-term goals. They want exactly what they want and they will settle for nothing less, which means that they will also completely avoid situations and people who try to stray them away from that path.

The number four knows what they want and they also recognize that they are the only ones responsible for their ability to actually get these things in life. For that reason, they rely heavily on themselves and they feel extremely frustrated and anxious if they are unable to rely on themselves for any given reason. In the event that they find themselves relying on other people to come through on helping them complete a plan or make something happen, or in the very rare event that they find themselves feeling emotionally dependent on another person, a four feels extremely out of place. This experience for a number four feels terrifying because, to them, this means that they are at risk of never fulfilling their goals which continues to be the single most important thing in a fours' life.

In addition to their drive and devotion, fours are also very much committed to being realistic and enjoying life as it is. They are practical, which means that they have an easy time accepting reality, regardless of what reality looks like for them. They love enjoying themselves and engaging in activities that let them build their skills or exercise their mind, especially if these activities have a clear goal or outcome. In other words, a four is more likely to prefer a game of golf or a night of bowling to a movie night, although they will happily tag along for a movie night if they know that their loved one really wants to go.

Four as A Name Number

Four energy in the name number position can be a complex and interesting energy as individuals with a number four here want to turn their relationships into something with clear goals. The four energy here already knows exactly what they want from a relationship and they will likely already have an image in their mind going into any relationship, whether it be a friendship or a romantic relationship. For that reason, they are likely going to have expectations which can be both a positive and negative experience in relationships. On one hand, having expectations going into relationships means that you know what you want and that you can avoid relationships where you are likely to be mistreated or mismatched to the person. On the other hand, the four energy can be very possessive over their expectations which may mean that you repeatedly end friendships or partnerships that do not match your insanely strict and potentially unreasonable expectations. You may find that you leave no room for mistakes or reality in your relationships, as much as you want to. In your mind you are okay with people being real and raw, but when it comes to the actual relationship itself you may be highly turned off by people who repeatedly miss the mark with your high expectations.

In positive relationships, you find a way to have realistic expectations and you set goals in the relationship that are not destructive. You find a way to find a sense of accomplishment through things like making your loved ones laugh on a regular basis, helping them feel supported and loved, and showing them that you care. Rather than having one single goal, you find goals that you can achieve over and over again so that you always have something to work toward, which keeps you feeling engaged and positive in your relationship. Once you have found these goals, you are very practical and realistic in your relationships which means that you are easy to please. People feel very peaceful around you because you give them a space where it feels safe to work on who they are and develop themselves in your presence.

In negative relationships, you may become a destructive force. You have a tendency to try to work on people or do the work for people, which leads to you feeling annoyed when they are not responsive. You either become frustrated when they do not change, or you realize that all of your hard work is not resulting in the payoff that you wished for so you are not feeling accomplished. Both of these scenarios feel like your worst nightmare, so you end up feeling completely rejected and disappointed in your relationships. You may also find that you have such a clear goal for your relationship that you will push through and try to make it happen regardless of what the other person wants. This could show up as wanting someone to be your best friend and expecting them to be there for you even when they don't want to be, or wanting someone to be your wife or husband even though they have clearly expressed that they are not ready or willing to marry you. Rather than accepting people's wishes and respecting them, you may instead try to force them into conforming into the person that you want them to be. Sometimes, people may feel like a charity case around you, or like they can never please you because you are always trying to change them.

Four as A Destiny Number

If you have a four as a destiny number, you are reaching a point of soul maturity. In this life cycle you are going to be working toward integrating life lessons and growing as a person, which means that your primary purpose in life is personal development. A four destiny path will often find that they connect to a specific vision and that vision is often related to their karmic path, or that which they have come to integrate in this lifetime.

Some four paths may find that their life lessons are more personal than what work can offer so they may be drawn to switch paths from time to time in their career as they gain what they were meant to gain and move on to gain the next piece of information. For example, they may work as a secretary to learn how to be of service, then work as a carpenter to learn how to invest in physical labor. Alternatively, a four life path may have one single plan for what they want in life and everything they do supports them in getting there. Often, this work will be very predictable and stable, but the details will change up so that the four destiny path does not get bored of the work. An example would be woodworking, where the four destiny path can make a new project each time but the tools and general structure of the career path remains the same the entire time.

When it comes to life lessons, the four is working on two very specific lessons: integrating their karmic lessons and maturing their spirituality. The number four may find themselves initially drawn to logic and reasoning early on in their life path, but over time they will begin to accept and become interested in the unexplainable and will likely want to explore it in depth. The four destiny path may prefer to avoid any types of spiritual growth that cause their reality to appear off or wrong, as this can disrupt the stability and anchor to reality that they crave. In other words, the more intense spiritual practices such as astral traveling and timeline hopping may seem interesting but ultimately far too unstable for the four destiny path. That being said, things like understanding meditation and the connection to the divine or intuitive connection will be fascinating and of interest to the four destiny path. They will want to put in the leg work to develop that connection and begin feeling the closeness so that they are able to better develop their spirituality and feel connected to their purpose.

Another big life lesson the four path needs to work on is being willing to let things go. The four destiny path grows extremely attached to what they want from life and what they expect to receive and they feel incredibly let down when they realize that what they want and what they are receiving is not one and the same. Again, the tendency to try and force people to change or force situations to become what they were looking for can happen which can lead to toxic behaviors of self-sabotage and occasionally manipulation toward others. Learning how to detach from desired outcomes so that they can still find happiness in life in general, whether it looks the way they wanted it to or not, will be vital for a number four destiny path.

CHAPTER 10
Number 5: The Adventurer

Number five energy is a very free, fun-loving energy that appreciates adventure. The number five energy is one that loves detachment, going with the flow, and experiencing all that life has to offer with an open mind. Five energies can be compared to a nomadic individual who finds the greatest joy in floating about and going wherever life takes them next. Let's dig deeper to learn more about what the number five energy is and how it affects chart readings.

Number Five Vibration

Number five is a feminine freedom seeking energy. Think of a goddess dancing through a field of flowers, with her hair flowing in the wind and her arms reaching out to brush through the wildflowers and you will have a fairly accurate understanding of what the five energy is like. The five is one that loves to experience life, and that has matured enough in its soul journey that it can experience life in a more open-hearted manner. At this point, the number five energy is more than halfway through its life cycle stages, so it has a clearer understanding around what life is and why it is here. Although the person with the five energy may not have a clear understanding of this information, the deeper awareness exists within their spirituality and manifests in their self-expression.

Five as A Psychic Number

If you have five as a psychic number, you are likely obsessed with travel blogs, adding travel pins to your Pinterest board, and filling up your passport with new stamps as often as possible. Fives love adventure and experiencing life, and they are passionate about getting out into the world and exploring every different type of experience that there is to have. A five psychic number equals a person who is the ultimate travel companion as they are typically up for any adventure, are great at being resourceful, and know how to surrender to the experience and allow it to be as enjoyable as possible. Although a five may have a travel itinerary for what they want to do, this itinerary is often just a guide so that they can feel confident that there will be plenty of adventure in their travels. Typically, the five will be willing to stay flexible with their itinerary as long as they get to have all of the most exciting experiences that they were looking forward to.

This type of flexible planning is not just present in official travels, but also tends to exist in the day to day life of a five, too. If you have five in your psychic number position, you likely enjoy making each day as memorable as possible by turning everything into an experience. You may find that you are always receiving invitations to join people on their adventures, and typically you are more than happy to oblige. Even just walking into your favorite corner store can lead to you meeting a cool traveler with a great story who wants to take you out for dinner so that you can engage in further conversation. Everything turns into an adventure with you because you literally attract this energy into your life.

You are deeply motivated by pleasure and you will often choose your life based on what feels pleasurable for you. Some may say that your life is irresponsible because you struggle to settle down or live life the traditional way because it simply does not bring enough stimulation to your life. Everything in your experience is just that: an experience. From the people you surround yourself with to the work that you engage in, you are always looking to make everything as fun as possible. You are likely drawn to making everything as fun as you can, such as by choosing to take on the career path of something more exciting like a tour guide or a tree planter, rather than a desk clerk or a banker. To you, the more adventurous and exciting every aspect of your life is, the better. Conventional lifestyles be damned.

In addition to your free-flowing, pleasure-seeking ways, you are also the type of person who always has something to talk about. You love telling stories, recalling your adventures, and sharing your experiences with other people. For you, talking about it feels like reliving it, and in many cases that is just as good as going on a great adventure. Plus, telling your own stories encourages people to tell theirs, which not only feels like you are living vicariously through them but also inspires you to plan your next adventure. Another element of this freedom reality is that you are likely deeply into natural and alternative health and healing. You are much more likely to sip a peppermint tea when you have an upset stomach than you are to take an antacid. You may even be idealistic at times about how life is and how life should be, and about how health and healing should look, sometimes believing that all aspects of a conventional life should be discarded in favor of a completely natural and freedom-based lifestyle.

Five as A Name Number

If you have the number five in your name number position, you are the type of person who loves free flowing relationships. You may find that you constantly have people coming and going from your life and that truly fixing into stable relationships is not exactly easy for you. Although you likely have a small circle of close friends, chances are your travels regularly bring you away from them so your friendship is typically online or through the phone more often than it is physical. You likely see these individuals every time you are in town, but chances are you are not worried about having some distance between you and them since you are certainly not a homebody. The one type of friend you may keep long term is one who is willing to become a travel buddy and join you on your adventures, but even then you are likely to flow apart at some point. Keeping a close relationship in your life can be somewhat challenging, though you will definitely do what you can to settle down with the right lover.

When it comes to love, you crave a lover who is going to be able to offer you the type of adventure and pleasure that you need from a relationship. Whether it is going to a new restaurant to try out a new type of food that you have never had before, or adventuring to a new place to romp around between the sheets, you love adventure and pleasure being mixed together. Unless you find a lover, who can weave together pleasure and adventure, however, it may be challenging for you to settle down. If your romantic relationship is healthy, it will likely be filled with sensuality, understanding, personal growth, surrender, companionship, variety, and experiences. This type of relationship serves you deeply, and as a result you feel the ability to show up fully. If you are in an unhealthy relationship for you, you may find that you become very detached and you struggle to show up in the relationship. Still, you may attempt to hold on if you feel that you are not receiving pleasure elsewhere in your life as this begins to feel like a place where you can at least get *something*. In other words: you are prone to settling because of how easy going you can be at times.

In friendships, there is a chance that all of your friends look drastically different from each other, and maybe even you. In a way, this kind of makes you all similar: because you are all so incredibly unique. You tend to spend more time with people who have interesting stories and complex personalities because these types of people give you something to dig into and understand. You enjoy trying to figure people out or, better yet, not being able to figure people out because they are just so different from you. Having this diversity keeps you feeling very engaged and fascinated by the people around you, which makes you feel fulfilled on a social level.

In both love and friendships, you may find that you are frequently flowing from relationship to relationship because of your freedom loving nature. You may have people who you don't talk to for months only to talk to them again like no time has passed, and for some that time may even be years. Others will come and go and you will cherish the memory but beyond a Facebook or Instagram like here and there you never see them again. Still, chances are that most of the people in your life inspire you in a big way and you admire them for all that they have added to your life. Each person you have connected with has, in one way or another, added value either by their stories they have shared, their wisdom, or the inspiration they offered you based on who they were. Everyone else seems to simply cease to exist.

Five as A Destiny Number

If you have five as a destiny number, your purpose in life is to discover how to enjoy a life of detachment, and maybe inspire other people to do the same thing along the way. Five destiny numbers tend to be the ones who spread the wisdom, although they may not necessarily fully understand and embody the wisdom in their own lives because of their natural detachment. (The embodiment of wisdom comes later in life path number seven.)

A five destiny number is often known for having grandiose visions of what they want the world to be like, and they may be very idealistic about how it can happen. They believe that the entire world can heal overnight, if only everyone were to get on board with the same things, and they often secretly hold onto the hope that this will happen in their lifetimes. Even though they are realistic enough to realize that it is unlikely, they will still hold hope that this will become their reality in their lifetime. In fact, they want it so much that they will often surround themselves with people who are willing to fit into this vision and so, at least in their world, it looks like this is happening.

For other people, this purpose of vision and idealism tends to spark inspiration that we can all slow down and take it easy and simply aim to get along. The five destiny path teaches others that it is okay to accept people as they are, and it is okay to detach from those who do not fit our lifestyles. Sometimes, the easiest way to create the life that we desire is to accept that we can have it and then continue working toward having it every single day.

A big life lesson for the number five destiny path is that, no matter how well they shape their own reality, an entire reality that is completely opposite to what they have created continues to exist. The number five life path can sometimes be irresponsible and willing to break rules and do as they please to fulfill their idealistic life vision, and this can lead to many problems in life. Some may find themselves in trouble with other people or even authorities because they have not honored the fact that the general reality is vastly different from what they long for. Another big lesson is going to be around commitment, as the number five life path tends to be the complete opposite of the number four life path. Where the number four tends to be attached and clingy, the number five tends to be detached sometimes to a complete fault. Learning how to detach without completely detaching will be necessary so that the number five can learn about commitment and consistency in life.

Without this, the number five may find themselves struggling to commit, engaging in infidelity, being dishonest to protect their freedom, and otherwise being unfair or disrespectful to the people around them in favor of their own pleasure.

CHAPTER 11
Number 6: The Harmonious Caregiver

The number six is a beautiful number that is really beginning to advance in terms of spiritual maturity. When you have number six energy into your chart, you are vibrating with the energy of the harmonious caregiver. The harmonious caregiver is one that loves balance and harmony and also has a tendency to want to nurture and care for those around them. This should not be mistaken for codependency or excessive giving, however, as the balanced harmonious caregiver is naturally nurturing without giving to the point of feeling personally depleted.

Number Six Vibration
The number six vibration is like that of a healthy and well-balanced mother: or the idealistic mother that no one ever truly becomes. This is the mother who bakes cookies, dresses nicely every day, gets her job done, pays the bills on time, spreads copious amounts of love to her children, and still has energy to be happy and positive at the end of each day. That type of energy is the energy that the harmonious caregiver vibrates at. Although the harmonious caregiver is unlikely to be able to do it all without feeling drained, they are able to do plenty and feel fulfilled through the act of giving. They love giving and being appreciated in return for their giving, as it helps them feel incredibly well-received by their loved ones and the people around them.

Six as A Psychic Number

If you have six as a psychic number, people may regularly refer to you as the "parent" of the group. You are likely the type of person who knows what is going on in all of their loved ones' lives and you will happily clear some time in your schedule to support in any way that you can. Not only will you give your time when it is needed, but you will also skillfully anticipate the need and offer your support before anyone even asks because you can recognize that other people need your care. "How are you?" is probably one of your most asked questions, and people seem to unleash their entire lives on you after you have asked because they feel safe with you. Even people who do not know you likely tell you their life story at random because they feel safe opening up to you. Intuitively, they can sense that you are a natural caregiver and that you are a safe person for them to share with.

You are an unconditional lover through and through, and in your balanced state you know just how to love unconditionally without harming yourself. You know how to love people unconditionally from a distance when necessary, and how to keep them close in your circle when it feels right. You can lovingly let go of people or situations that are not fit for you without harboring any ill feelings or resentment toward the individual or the situation because you know that deep down everyone means well and every situation was created out of positive intentions. Although some people may be incapable of carrying everything out in a positive and thoughtful manner, you know that they rarely truly meant to cause any harm.

In addition to how you care for and show up for others, you are also the type of person who is deeply into being of service. You have likely volunteered plenty, either through a traditional volunteer where you signed up as a volunteer and offered your services, or through a situation where you volunteered unconventionally. This could look like anything from volunteering to hold the door open to taking a homeless person out to lunch with you so that you can fill their stomach with food. Chances are, you have done both and you do both regularly.

Sixes are not just about the more feminine style of service, either, as they are also known for offering protection and stability when people need it. A six is not afraid to be your safe space and protect you from anything that you are going through, or from yourself if you need it. They will always do their best to step in and make sure that everyone feels stable and grounded because they know how vital this is to the human experience. To them, they want everyone to genuinely feel good in life.

In their personal time when a six is not being of service to someone else, they are likely offering themselves the same acts of service. While it can sometimes take convincing for them to realize that they deserve the same level of care, once they do a six will happily spend their downtime engaging in self-care so that they can feel fulfilled and protected as well. They do this knowing that it feels good to be of service, knowing the value of being on both the giving and receiving end of the service, and realizing that this helps them have a full cup so that they can be of even more service to others.

Truly, everything in a sixes life is about caregiving in one way or another, regardless of who the recipient is.

Six as A Name Number

If you have six as a name number, your relationships likely consist of you begin the caretaker to your friends and loved ones. You have a high passion for looking after the ones you love, and you will always go out of your way to help them feel cherished and cared for. You are probably the type of friend to bring them gifts, to send them "thinking about you" messages, and to offer to take a friend out when you know they have had a particularly challenging day. You like to offer emotional support as well as physical support, either by being a shoulder to cry on or a friend that your friends can rely on to help them with a task like moving or getting their kids to school on time.

In love, you favor relationships where you are able to take care of the other person, and you likely also enjoy being taken care of. In your ideal relationship dynamic, chances are you have a vision of you and your partner each taking care of each other in your own unique ways. You may be likely to want to appoint a certain type of caretaking to each partner, such as you taking care of making meals for the two of you and your partner taking care of cleaning up after them. You are very selfless in relationships so it is ideal for you to enter relationships with people who will also be very selfless, or at least those who will respect your tendency to be selfless and who will not ask too much of you. In some scenarios, your selflessness can become a potential problem for you if you fail to learn how to create boundaries. Unfortunately, some people may take advantage of your selflessness by asking too much of you or by frequently taking from you, which can result in a relationship where you feel taken advantage of and neglected. This unhealthy dynamic can lower your self-esteem and self-confidence in a big way as it makes one of your unique and most valued traits about yourself out to be something bad. Avoiding relationships with people who cannot be empathetic and caring toward you in return is ideal to ensure that you can enjoy a harmonious relationship with your partner.

In friendships, you may often be looked to as the caring one in your friend group. People know that they can rely on you in many different ways and so they tend to want to keep you in their lives for the long haul. They love how you are always willing to show up in relationships and play equally, how you genuinely care about them, and how your compassion is authentic and sincere. To many people, the depth of your care for them is inspiring and helps them feel like they matter, which is an important quality in their eyes. Being able to offer this to your friends is a valuable asset. However, just like with your romantic relationships, you have to be cautious about accumulating friends who ask for too much or who are not considerate about the amount that you do for them. Being unappreciated or taken advantage of is a big risk factor for you and it can feel extremely painful when it happens. Seek to have strong boundaries so that you can find friends who are also empathetic and caring. Once you do, you will have found friends who you can keep for life, which is likely going to be extremely refreshing for you.

Six as A Destiny Number

If you have six as a destiny number, you have come here with a huge gift that you share with the world. These days, our world is known for being cruel and heartless, and you are just the opposite of that which means that you possess the very qualities that we need more of in this world. Your sensitivity and compassion may feel like a burden to you at times because it may not always be reciprocated by other people, but know that your very way of living is healing for the collective. Your ability to be genuine, to care about others, and to share your comfort and wisdom with those around you is very healing to the people that you engage with. You may find yourself being drawn into a career path that allows you to nurture others and share this caretaking energy around so that more people can receive it. You seem to intuitively know that just being in the presence of your care and compassion is healing, and so you do your best to pursue a career path that allows you to offer this energy to as many people as possible. You are likely to become a childcare provider, a therapist, a nurse, a retirement home care aid, or something similar that allows you to care for others, especially when those others are particularly vulnerable to the risks of the current state of society.

Your life lessons are likely going to revolve around learning that not everyone is like you, and around learning how to have boundaries and take care of yourself. You need to realize that not everyone is going to be as compassionate and genuine as you are, so you are going to need to refine your intuition to ensure that you are always trusting in people who are genuinely trustworthy. Be willing to admit that not everyone is as nice as you know they could be, and avoid letting those who show that they are not nice have the space to harm you. Giving unkind people an all-access pass to your life by keeping them as friends or lovers can expose you to the risks of being a kind-hearted person that gets taken advantage of. Even in your healthy friendships, exercising boundaries will be important to ensure that you are not taking on too much. You do not want to constantly be taking care of everyone in your life, no matter how much you enjoy it, as sometimes you are going to need to take care of yourself. Asserting your boundaries will ensure that you only maintain friendships or relationships with people who are able to respect you as you are and not take advantage of you.

As well, you really need to lean into understanding that you are just as deserving of your own care as anyone else is. You need to overcome your tendency to put your needs second to the needs of everyone else so that you can start taking better care of yourself. Admit when things are too much, be willing to say no when you need to, and release the belief that you have to do everything for everyone because that is simply not true. It is not selfish, bad, or wrong to want or need to do things for yourself before you can do things for yourself. In fact, it is completely normal. Be as caring toward yourself as you are toward others and you will strike a great balance that allows you to nurture your caretaking tendencies without causing mental or emotional pain to yourself along the way.

CHAPTER 12
Number 7: The Truth-Seeker And Wise One

The number seven is a very sociable and collective-based number. This number is frequently used to share about the vibe of the "collective" or of all humans who are presently living on Earth. This number is a very deep, contemplative number that is known to vibrate with energies of wisdom, knowledge, and truth. To learn more about what a seven in your chart means, read on!

Number Seven Vibration

To get a strong understanding of what a seven vibrates at, think about a wise elder who possesses knowledge from life experience and soul searching. This is an elder who has spent their entire life seeking to understand life itself as well as other people and how the entire world seems to work. They possess knowledge about everything from love and human connections to the rising and setting of the sun each day, and they are generally willing to pass this knowledge around freely to anyone who seeks to learn it. This elder values the truth and they will often see right through anything that is not inherently true, as if it is their gift. Despite how much this elder knows, they openly acknowledge that they do not know everything and so they are always curious and open to learning more from those around them. This elder possesses everything that is relevant to the number seven vibration. Words that frequently resonate with a number seven energy include: wisdom, deep contemplation, inner-selves, isolation, philosophy, awareness, mysticism, emotions, understanding, and discernment.

Seven as A Psychic Number

If you have a seven as a psychic number, you likely identify as a bit of a loner. You may frequently be seen as an introvert because of how much you enjoy your alone time and how willing you are to do things by yourself. Traveling alone, dining alone, and living alone do not scare you in the slightest because you are truly open to what being alone has to offer. Despite how much you enjoy your alone time, however, you are certainly not antisocial or against being around people. In fact, being around people gives you plenty to contemplate when you are alone later on, so you likely enjoy a fairly healthy balance between being around other people and being alone.

You have a tendency to avoid labelling yourself, especially when that label creates any level of restriction in your life. You see how vast and beautiful life is and you believe that the idea of attempting to fit ourselves into confined boxes with labels is heinous. Instead of trying to fit yourself into a box, you would much rather see yourself living freely and moving from day to day without trying to put any restrictions on anything. This non-restrictive way of living gives you plenty of freedom to discover more about life, thus leaving you open to learning about new information or new ways of life that you may not have considered in the past. In your opinion, the more relaxed and fluid your life is, the more you can remain open to the world around you, and that is your ultimate goal.

You prefer to live a life of truth, so you are unlikely to hold back your opinions or your true beliefs. That being said, you are very discerning so sometimes you will keep your truth to yourself and simply live in alignment with it rather than telling everyone. You do not feel a great need to tell everyone what you are going through in life at all times because you do not feel it is necessary. You would prefer to only share information that is relevant or that can genuinely support people, as this feels like a more worthwhile investment of your time. For that reason, you likely do not spend very much time engaging on social media because it likely seems fairly mindless to you. You would much rather be engaged in an interesting conversation with someone who can teach you something, or who you can teach something to, or invested in a great book.

You likely spend your time ingesting and recording your knowledge, either through writing or through studying. Sitting in quiet contemplation is a good time to you, so you may not understand why everyone in the modern world seems to be in such a rush all the time. To you, sitting quietly on your couch staring out the window seems just as fun as going to the movies or getting dinner with your friends. During your quiet time you reflect on knowledge that you have gained and put together your own beliefs and understandings about the world around you so that you can make even more sense of life and humanity. This activity feels necessary to you as this is how you are able to make sense of the world around you, so you likely invest plenty of time into this activity on a daily basis. If you do not get this alone time, you may find that you feel agitated and overwhelmed by everyone around you, which may lead to you wanting to retreat for a while. If you find that you are surrounded by people who fail to recognize this or respect this, you may be likely to go into a deep state of introspection and introversion to avoid people who are not respecting you.

Seven as A Name Number

If you have seven as a name number, your relationships are likely very deep and reflective. Chances are you surround yourself with people who can teach you something, or who you can teach something to, although it is more likely that each person fits both of these descriptions. You value relationships that revolve around personal growth and development, and you love watching your friends learn and grow. You likely meet people in places like schools, study groups, museums or art galleries, or in other places that are rich with information and history that you can learn about. You also tend to spend your time in places like this with your friends or lovers as this is your ideal hangout spot.

In love, you are likely a very deep lover. You are thoughtful of the person you share your love with, and you genuinely put the energy into getting to know who they are and what they love about life. You like getting to know your partner thoroughly as, in your opinion, knowing each other completely is one of the deepest forms of intimacy that you can engage in. Complete knowingness and understanding feels like a privilege to you, and so you are likely going to be cautious to ensure that the people you invite into your romantic life are actually willing to engage in this type of intimacy. You are highly turned on by hours of talking and educating each other, fact-checking together, and playing games that revolve around trivia in one way or another. You enjoy growing and learning together and will feel the most attraction and affection toward people who place a high value on these two qualities of your relationship as well. You may at times come off as detached or uninvolved in love which is largely because of the fact that you are more logical and analytical than you are emotional which means that you may have a hard time physically showing your emotions. To you, engaging in healthy debates or going to study sessions together is an ideal way of showing love to another person, so it may feel unnatural for you to show love in other ways such as by spending afternoons watching movies or engaging in seemingly mindless fun together.

In friendships, you are likely deeply connected to very few people. You believe in quality over quantity and you would much rather spend your whole life getting to completely know a handful of people rather than spend your whole life only partially getting to know many different people. Once you have people who you are close to, however, you will also likely find yourself engaging freely in conversations with other individuals who are extremely knowledgeable. You could make acquaintances with a museum director and talk for hours about the exhibits and how they were created, as this type of engagement feels extremely enjoyable to you. However, unless this person really feels worthy of your time and energy they will often only remain acquaintances or passing ships in the night as you gain some information and move on, never to speak to them again. You are very particular about your close circle of friends and you do not want to waste time with people. You tend to attract friends who are just as deep and introspective as you are, as these are the individuals who truly get you and who you truly get, too. That being said, chances are not everyone in your social circle will be as deep as you are because this may feel boring and redundant. Instead, you are likely to attract friends who are deep and fascinated by complex things, and who also have fairly complex personalities in general. This way, you can spend a lifetime getting to know them and being entertained and fascinated by the very different way that they carry themselves through life.

Seven as A Destiny Number

If you have seven as a destiny number, you are committed to your purpose of being a truth seeker. Seven destiny numbers are drawn to any career path that serves the purpose of gaining and sharing knowledge with others, so they will often become yogis, teachers, educators, tour guides, museum directors, historians, or anything else that serves their need to constantly be learning more. In your eyes, a career that always has room for learning and growing is the perfect position for you to be in. You want to master things, but you also want to have plenty to master so that you never tire from the work that you do.

You are also likely passionate about truth-seeking in general, so you may find yourself feeling drawn to being the type of individual who educates the public about the truth as you see it. You like to inform people about corporate greed, the reality of where their clothes and food come from, and the government's latest antics. You are also likely sharing interesting facts or tidbits of information that fascinate other people simply because this interests you. You feel that it is your duty to make sure that the public is informed, or at the very least that your family and friends are informed, so you make it your mission to stay informed yourself and spread that information around. You may sometimes be called a conspiracy theorist or someone who is overly paranoid because of how open you are to realizing the truth behind things that many people simply ignore.

A big life lesson for you is going to be to learn when to share and when not to. While discernment is likely one of your qualities, you may find that you tend to discern based on what feels right for you as opposed to what feels right for the situation. For this reason, you may share when it is not ideal to share and keep to yourself when it would make more sense to be open and honest. You are also prone to pessimism and anti-socialness, particularly if you use your detective skills to dig too deep into conspiracy theories and the likes. You may find yourself at risk of believing that the world is a terrible place and that people are selfish and greedy, and you may take on a very jaded view of the world in general. Learning how to overcome this jaded view is a valuable opportunity for you to stay open-minded and truly enjoy life for what it is, rather than getting yourself down over every little thing. Learn how to be open to learning about the truth without attaching so much personal emotion to it so that you can inform yourself without depressing yourself.

CHAPTER 13
Number 8: The Strong Leader

The number eight is a powerful influential number that possesses incredibly strong qualities. The eight is an authoritative number that is known to be rich with abundance and prosperity of all types. Eights are about material freedom, success, and money. If you have an eight in your chart, you can learn more about what that means about you here!

Number Eight Vibration
By the time we reach number eight in the numerological sequence, we have reached a point of intense spiritual maturity. We have also reached the point where a person is going to want to start enjoying life for what it is because they have achieved plenty in the spiritual realms. Eights are confident, love all that life has to offer, and want to experience everything that was placed on Earth to the finest degree. The vibration of eight recognizes that everything was put on Earth for us to experience and has officially reached the point where they can learn how to experience these things in good taste. They are generally not greedy or selfish, nor will they acquire their success at any cost because they have learned how to do it in a way that is good for everyone involved. That being said, the eight also knows what they want and is shameless about wanting to enjoy the finer things in life.

Eight as A Psychic Number

If you have eight as your psychic number, you likely value influence, authority, and personal power. An individual who is in control of themselves, who is unafraid to take charge in a situation, and who has a strong air of confidence to them, you are someone who truly enjoys the finer things in life. You have a good sense of judgment when it comes to most things in life and you fancy yourself an "old soul" because even when you don't know, you know. To you, most types of wisdom are more about common sense than anything else because you find yourself seeming to already know things that other people are just beginning to understand. You are unshakeable.

You have a deep desire for everything to be right in the world, so you often exercise your leadership skills and personal power as an opportunity for you to do things that serve the collective. You will always go out of your way to serve in a peaceful way, and you are sometimes considered a humanitarian because you genuinely want to see everything that is good with the world grow while everything else falls off. You are conscious, honorable, and are highly ambitious in all that you do in life. You have a knack for gaining insight into situations and this makes you excellent at planning things, including things that involve large groups of people. Leading people and achieving success in your leadership and with your team comes naturally to you, it's almost like you do not even have to try.

You are rooted deep in reality and have come to understand that the world is your playground and it is perfectly safe for you to enjoy it. At this point you have enough understanding of how life works and what life is that you can easily feel confident and safe in virtually any situation. If you are not careful, however, you may begin to develop a superiority complex as you believe that you know more than others and that you are stronger than they are. This can lead to egotism and irritability as you attempt to get other people to follow your lead, especially when they are not willingly doing so. Rather than respecting other peoples' right to say no, you may instead try to push yourself on them and force them into seeing that you clearly know more.

Number eight resonates with the energy of karma, so you may find yourself making good on a lot of your karma in this life cycle. You may also find that you now possess all of the knowledge and skill that you need to neutralize this karma effectively, so while it is painful and challenging you seem to be strong enough to handle virtually anything that comes your way. Each time you effectively overcome a hardship, you inevitably begin to feel even stronger and see this as being an asset to your overall leadership qualities. For that reason, no matter how challenging the lesson may be, you generally look back on them as being positive lessons that you are grateful to have had the opportunity to learn in your lifetime. To you, almost nothing is more than you can handle, and when it feels too much you can be extremely resourceful and practical about getting the help you need to navigate the challenge. This is why you tend to be so powerful: because you can call in added strength from your resources when you feel that you cannot single-handedly do it yourself, assuming that you have evolved enough to be willing to admit the need for help and ask for it when it is needed.

Eight as A Name Number

If you have eight as a name number, you are likely very strong in your relationships. You value relationships that are about flash and material goods, so you are likely wanting love and friendships that look good to the eye. You want to be going to the hottest clubs, eating at the best restaurants, spending time with people who dress as nicely as you, and growing your reputation through the people that you hang out with. While you are likely nice to everyone, you surround yourself with people who are conscious about how they look and how they show up in the world because these are people who represent themselves well, which means that they will represent you well, too. You want your relationships to be filled with abundance, consideration, wisdom, and growth. Sometimes, you may be considered egotistical in relationships because of how much value you place on the way things look and feel.

In love, you are likely going to find yourself choosing partners based on appearances over character, which may lead to trouble. You like a person who looks good and who cares about how your relationship appears to others, which can sometimes lead you into relationships with arrogant people who are not as good as they look on paper. When you do find someone who is genuine and flashy like you, however, your relationship is likely going to be the kind that people gush over on social media. You will both dress nicely and keep your appearances up, both for yourselves and as a way to show respect to each other. Together you rule the world through your integrity, your passion for material possessions, and your understanding of how to have a good life in general. You both tend to be very patient with each other, while also being big motivators in helping each other achieve your dreams in life. When you unite in a positive partnership, you both are highly ambitious and you become as protective over your partner's dream as you are over your own. You will do everything you can to advance your own dream as well as your partners dream because you want both of you to enjoy in prosperity and abundance.

When it comes to friendships, you may come across as picky because you truly do not want to spend your time around people who are not concerned with how they look or how they come across to the people around them. People who appear unkempt, lazy, or rude are a big turn off to you and you are likely going to avoid keeping these people around for long. You tend to run with the "elite" circle, you like people who dress nicely, who genuinely care about humanity, and who are very considerate about how they speak and what they are saying to people with their words and their behaviors. The better your friends look, the better you look, and that is very important to you. You want all of you to come across in a positive way so that you can feel confident that you are all promoting each other's growth and ability to enjoy a fine life, rather than holding each other back.

Because of how much emphasis you place on physical appearances and the way people present themselves, you may find yourself having a hard time accumulating a social circle unless you are willing to really put yourself out there. Some eights find themselves in a perpetual state of loneliness because their standards are too high for the average person and they are not always willing to or capable of getting in with crowds that appear to have higher standards. Alternatively, the eight name number individual may have had so many unwanted run-ins with egotistical people that they are now jaded and have a hard time trusting that anyone is as good as they say they are. They may keep everyone at an arms' length for fear of letting anyone in and later regretting it.

Eight as A Destiny Number

If you have eight as a destiny number, you are likely here to serve the purpose of showing people that there is nothing wrong with enjoying the finer things in life. You love showing people how to enjoy riches, dress themselves in luxury, and shamelessly welcome material possessions and wealth into their lives. You live to demolish the belief that being wealthy means that you are inherently a greedy and rude person because you want everyone to see that they can have a nice life without it meaning that they are a bad person. Chances are you are going to pursue a career path that works with money or something considered to be luxurious or wealthy in one way or another. You may find yourself drawn to being a banker, a money coach or financial advisor, a wealth guide, a manager of a high-end designer store, a high-end designer, or even a luxury travel agent. Anything to do with riches, luxury, and the finer life is attractive to you in this lifetime.

A big lesson you are going to have to be mindful of learning is that not everyone is as enthralled by opulence as you are, and you are going to have to realize that this is not a bad thing. There is no reason why everyone should have to be driven by the same things as you are, so learning to accept people for their preferences and being willing to be patient with people who are not as attracted to wealth as you are is important. Be cautious about your tendency to bring your ego into things as this will hold you back in a big way. Learn how to be willing to acknowledge when you are not aligned with someone and simply recognize it as a misalignment rather than judging them as being low class or in some way beneath you. This is a valuable way for you to hold value and respect for everyone without feeling obligated to spend your time with people who do not feel like a good fit for you.

You also need to be cautious about your tendency to believe that you know more than other people or that you are better than other people based on your knowledge. Because you have reached a lifetime where you have a larger amount of spiritual maturity, you may find yourself running into situations where you become close-minded or even like a dictator in your life because of how superior you may feel. Learning to stay open-minded and remembering that you are not the ruler of the world is powerful. You may feel that confident in life, but refrain from allowing that level of confidence to lead you to a point where you feel like you have nothing more to learn and no room for growth in life. Stay humble and always be willing to learn more than what you already know.

CHAPTER 14
Number 9: The Humanitarian

The number nine is a number of faith, service to humanity, and spiritual maturity. People who have a nine anywhere in their chart are resonating at a high level of spiritual maturity, or they have access to a high level of spiritual maturity. These individuals crave self-love, self-expression, compassion, freedom, and influence. They have a tendency to be very idealistic and, if they take the time to develop themselves effectively, they can become the type of person that many other people naturally look up to based off of their very nature. To learn more about what a number nine in your chart says about who you are, read on!

Number Nine Vibration
A number nine resonates with the energy of maturity and sovereignty. This is the final number in the single digits, which translates to the end of a cycle in numerology. Number nine energy is very sophisticated in that this energy is independent and capable. Number nine energy is an embodiment type of energy, where the people who exist within number nine tend to *be*. Rather than preaching wisdom, they *are* wise. Rather than exuding confidence, they *are* confident. Rather than calling in abundance, they *are* abundant. Nine energy is very integrated and embodied, which means that having a nine anywhere in your chart suggests that not only are you experiencing things relevant to that part of your chart in your life, but you are also deeply embodying them. This is a

86

highly valuable quality that many people long for, so having a nine in your chart suggests that you have a level of maturity and sovereignty that most people can only dream of having.

Nine as A Psychic Number

If you have a nine as your psychic number, you are likely a very poised human. You do not have to think too much about what to do or how to do it because most things simply come very naturally to you in your life. You are highly intuitive, sensitive, empathic, and awake. You are naturally tapped into a deeper level of Divine wisdom and mysticism than most, although that does not necessarily guarantee that you are going to be involved in Divinity or mystical practices. Still, there is a good chance that you have a natural affinity for them and that you are intuitively drawn into trying them out. Whenever you learn about something to do with spirituality or Divinity, you likely feel as though you already knew this information on some level and it is just being brought into your realm of awareness at this point. That being said, you may grow hungry to learn more as you become eager to let even more seep into your realm of awareness.

As an individual who has access to the highest embodiment of all, you are likely highly drawn to being tapped into acts of humanitarianism. Philanthropy, charity, and self-sacrifice come easy to you, and to you they do not feel like something you have to do because they are an inherent part of who you are. It comes naturally to you to fight for the underdog, advocate for those in need, and offer the shirt off your back if someone needs it more than you do. These do not feel like heroic acts, so it may surprise you when people treat you like you are some form of hero toward others. In your reality, this is simply how the world is supposed to work and you are only doing what you are meant to do as a citizen of the globe.

You tend to come across as very eccentric and people may be rather curious about you. Somehow, to them, you seem to embody the qualities of the perfect human which can often land you in the position of becoming a role model or an idol. People may even look to you to be their mentor because you embody many of the characteristics that are believed to be ideal and they want to learn how to do better, too.

Your character is deeply refined and is something that just *is*. The people around you can feel that you are not average and may feel like they know you well even when they do not know you at all because you exude a very clear sense of self. You rarely question who you are or what you are here to do because you can feel your sense of duty so deeply in your bones. Regardless of what path you take in life, you feel it to be a part of you as opposed to just a path that you walk to get to your desired destination. In addition to embodying who and what you are, you have also embodied the reality of the journey being equally as important as the destination, if not more so. You are the true definition of an old soul, and everyone around you can sense these sometimes even long before you can.

Nine as A Name Number

If you have nine as a name number, your relationships are likely rooted in service. While you like to be of service to the people in your life, you like even more to be of service together with the people in your life. In other words, you are highly attracted to people who are just as giving and philanthropic as you are. People who express an awareness of how their actions impact others and how they can serve others so that everyone can have access to a high quality of life are highly admirable to you and you will do all that you can to surround yourself with people like this. You likely meet your friends and lovers at charity events or volunteer gigs, as this is where you are likely to find people who are as devoted to service and humanitarianism as you are.

In love, you find the deepest of connections with people who will go to any length to serve in the world. Your ideal relationship is likely with someone who would happily hop aboard a flight to a third world country with you to help build a community or support people who are having a hard time with quality of life. Your favorite dates are those where you head to fancy charity galas or even out working the trenches at an animal welfare event. You are attracted to people who are passionate, giving, and dedicated to their work, because these are the types of individuals who can relate deeply to you. When it comes to acts of romance, you are turned on by people who are generous, creative, and raw or real. You prefer a true human who is willing to own their less-than-perfect realness to a human who tries to fake like they are better than they are. You are likely to be the type of person who is more impressed and flattered by what a gift means to the other person over what it means to you. For example, someone who is obsessed with books buying you a book will feel like a very big deal even if you are not a big reader because you know how meaningful that is to the person who gifted it to you. You are also grateful to partners who are accepting of your independence and who gracefully enjoy their own freedom while also offer you your own freedom without any pressure. The more you feel that you can be true to yourself in a relationship, the easier it is for you to be true to the other person, too.

In friendships, you value people who are willing to be as devoted to charity and service as you are as well. You are inspired by friends who are as passionate as you are, if not more so, and you likely spend a lot of time with your friends dreaming up charities that you could start and discussing possible solutions to worldwide problems like hunger or animal cruelty. You and your friends are very much on the same page about wanting to see the world become a better place and you embody this desire by actively trying to make it a better place every single day. You are drawn to people who are empathic, compassionate, and responsible. Your friends are likely a mixture of eco-friendly vegans who are often educating others on how they can be better global citizens and how they can support the world in becoming a better place. Your friends probably do not fit into the social norms, avoid designer and brand name products because they are often linked to being bad for the planet, and are people who tend to have a lot going on because they have a hard time saying "no" to helping out others. Although they are an array of different characters, at the core they all want the same thing: a safe and healthy environment for every living being on Earth.

Nine as A Destiny Number

If you have number nine as a destiny number, your purpose in life likely revolves around humanitarianism, philanthropy, and service to others. If you are not running a nonprofit, you are likely working at a job that gives back in some way, or working at the best paying job that you could find so that you can give your own money back to the causes that you believe in. In one way or another, all of your work revolves around giving back to the causes that are closest to your heart. You likely find that your cause is not only something that you are passionate about when it comes to work, but within your whole life, so this cause truly does become your purpose in life. Whether you are fighting for animal welfare or for better living conditions in third world countries, you are deeply passionate about what you do and you will do it with as much of your time and resources as possible.

In life, you have a big purpose to yourself, too, of closing up any lessons you have left to learn. You are at a point in your spiritual maturity where you need to be very aware of the lessons that you have been learning so that you can bring them to completion. This is only going to further your embodiment and ability to be the best that you can be, allowing you to engage even more with the life around you. Finalizing these lessons will also bring a deep sense of closure, clarity, and peace into your life so that you can start truly and deeply enjoying your life to the fullest. This does not mean that life will come easy for you or that you will not have any further lessons or challenges, but it does mean that you will start having an easier time moving through these challenges from a more whole state of being.

A big challenge you will likely have to overcome in life is learning that not everyone is as giving as you are, and learning to be okay with that. You may find yourself getting angry with people who do not support or understand your cause and this can lead to you feeling very pessimistic and angry with the world in general. You could become passionate to the point of being cruel or mean toward other people when they do not agree with you, which would be unfair. You want to make sure that you are staying passionate without stepping into other peoples' rights or being cruel about what you believe in. Remembering the saying "you catch more flies with honey than with vinegar" is an important saying here.

CHAPTER 15
Double-Digit Numbers And Master Numbers

In numerology, there are certain meanings that can be achieved through double-digits and master numbers, or repeating double-digits like 11, 22, 33, and so on. Although in most scenarios we want to break numbers down into a single number, sometimes leaving them whole or reading them whole as well as reading their sum can give us more information about what they mean. In this chapter you are going to learn about what double-digits and master numbers mean and how you can interpret them in numerology readings. You will also learn about when double-digits should be left alone and when they should be condensed into one single number to be read.

Double-Digit Meanings
Rarely will we keep a double-digit intact in numerology unless there is a very good reason to do so. An example would be if you are seeing a double-digit number everywhere, in which case it is likely that this combination has a specific message for you. For example, if you are seeing "42" everywhere then the energies associated with the number 4 and 2 combined may be very relevant to you at this time in your life. Unless you are seeing a double-digit number repeating like this, there is only one other time that a double-digit number will matter, and that is when there is a double-digit number that is condensed into a single digit number. For example, if you combine 5+4 to get 9, then you can use the

energy of 5 and 4 to better interpret what this particular 9 energy is going to be like. Chances are, it will be quite different from the energy of a 9 that is created from 1+8 or 3+6. In this situation, you are not actually reading just a double-digit so much as you are reading the deeper energy behind a single digit, though.

To give you a clearer understanding of what I mean, here are a few different interpretations of 9 energy based on the combinations above:

9 = 5+4: This particular nine energy is likely linked to work and adventure, meaning that the person is likely a humanitarian who wants to travel to volunteer and work with their hands. This particular humanitarian is more likely to be found digging wells for drinking water or building shelters for the homeless rather than playing treasurer at a fundraising event.

9 = 1+8: This particular humanitarian is likely a leader and is very strong, so they are more likely to be a project manager. They are going to be the ones who run their own charities or who run teams as non-profit leaders who keep everyone else in order. They are responsible for scheduling, planning events, keeping everything running, and directing the organization to success in achieving their charitable goals.

9 = 3+6: This humanitarian is more likely to show up as a creative caregiver. They want to be the ones who are helping the children, the elderly, or anyone else who would thoroughly enjoy their creative and expressive ways. This way, they can take care of others and express themselves in a fun way, which ultimately adds to their ability to give back.

As you can see, each of these nine energies are humanitarians as you would expect, but how they show up as a humanitarian is influenced by the double-digit number that produced their nine energy. Using double-digits in this way can help add more clarity and depth to your chart so that you can really get a clearer feel for who you are and what you are creating in life. If you do not fully identify with what you have been shown from your primary number, look at your secondary double-digit numbers and see how you may identify with them. This may guide to you having a clearer understanding of who you are and how you can pursue your core energy in a way that actually feels good for you.

Master Numbers
Master numbers are repeating double-digit numbers, from 11 to 99. Triple, quadruple, and higher digits of master numbers are considered to be repeating master numbers and you can learn more about those particular master number styles below in "Repeating Master Numbers."

Master numbers are said to hold amplified energy of the single digit numbers that they are connected to, as well as some of their own meanings altogether. If you have a master number show up in your reading, you never break it down to a single digit number as it is considered a sacred number all on its own. Below is a summary of what each master number means if it shows up for you in a reading.

Master Number 11: This master number is often considered to be the number of angels or of the Divine and is said to have a connection to a high state of spiritual evolution. If you are connected to master number 11, you are highly connected through your intuition and you are being divinely guided in the highest way possible. This is one of the most pure numbers on the planet.

Master Number 22: This number is associated with the number of the master builder and therefore resembles creativity and design. If you have number 22 show up for you, you have the energy behind you to manifest even the biggest life dreams that you may have. The master number 22 is typically only retained as a master number if it shows up in your numerology chart. If it shows up elsewhere, you should reduce this number to a number four energy.

Master Number 33: The master number 33 is known for being the master teacher and it also tends to hold great value in many different religions. This number revolves around peace and harmony, as well as creative expression. The meanings of both 3 and 6 will come through in the meaning of this number, as it resonates with both.

Master Number 44: This is actually one of the more rare master numbers, and when it presents itself it represents the master healer. This number has a high vibrational energy when it comes towards work and strength which makes it a powerful number for healing. A person who gets number 44 in their chart is likely relaxed, quick-witted, and very down to Earth.

Master Number 55: Those with master number 55 in their chart are extremely independent and determined, and they also crave adventure. 55 equals 10 which breaks down to 1, so a person with this number in their chart is likely going to want to travel through life on their own. They may have a hard time connecting with people long-term because of how much they value their personal freedom.

Master Number 66: The master number 66 is the number of transformation. At this energy, people are bringing in a lot of transformation and powerful knowledge. A person with a 66 in their chart craves justice, is highly compassionate, has a very optimistic outlook on life, and likely wants to live a life of perfection. They can also be very idealistic.

Master Number 77: This master number is the master number of intuition. A person with 77 in their chart is perfectly aligned to connect with higher planes of wisdom and act as a prophet of sorts for the collective. These individuals are naturally intuitive and will likely not have to work very hard to listen to and align with their intuition. They find it easy to stay connected to their intuition and follow it, and may find themselves feeling very out of place if they try to deny their intuition in any way.

Master Number 88: Master number 88 is an extremely powerful number to have in business, particularly in a business that needs to be run with masculine energy. A business that requires a strong lead will value from having a leader who aligns with master number 88 energy. This energy is analytical and efficient and likes to see things done properly and in a timely manner.

Master Number 99: Master number 99 resonates with embodiment, leadership, and wisdom. If you are aligned with master number 99, you should use this as a sign to embody your leadership qualities and your wisdom to help you guide other people through life. The deeper you embody these two qualities, the more at peace you are going to feel in your life.

Repeating Master Numbers
If you get repeating master numbers, or master numbers that align with three or more of the same number, you should take this as a sign of the energy being extremely amplified with that master number. The more a number repeats itself around you, the more intense that energy is for you and the more you need to pay attention and integrate the lessons of that number. Repeating master numbers can show up through two different repetition

patterns: through having multiple digits in one single space, or through showing up for you multiple times over a span of time.

If you see multiple numbers in a single space, such as 3 sets of master number 11 back to back or the master number 11 three different times in a contract in significant places, then you should know that the master number 11 energy is strong with that particular thing. This does not necessarily mean that the energy will be strong everywhere in your life, but in that particular area of your life you should pay close attention and focus on how you can integrate the lessons or energy of master number 11. In most cases when you oblige you will find that things run far more smoothly for you than they would have if you had ignored the sign altogether.

If you see a repeating number in many different places over a span of time, this means that this energy needs to be embodied more in your life in general. A common example people point out of this is seeing 11:11 everywhere. You may be intuitively drawn to look at the clock at 11:11 every day, see 11 in your daily life on a regular basis, and even have it show up randomly such as in your grocery bill or your friend's new phone number. If you feel like the number seems to be following you, it is because that particular number has an energy that you need to embody more of in your life.

PART 3
Numbers And Life

CHAPTER 16
Numbers For...

In addition to using numbers to learn more about yourself, you can also use numbers to align you with more of what you want in life. Numerology can be used to increase everything from financial abundance to the balance that you feel in life. Using numerology for these parts of your life can be a fun way to manifest more of what you want and align yourself with more of what makes you happy in life. In this chapter, you are going to learn about how you can use numerology to enhance your life.

Numbers for Money

Each of us has our own number for money in life. Money's number resonates with one, so you can find your money number by taking your psychic number, adding one into the equation, and breaking it down into a single digit. Below is a great example of how you can achieve your money number using the sample birthday of September 14, 1957.

Birthday Numbers Plus Money Number: 09, 14, 1957, 1

Equation: 0+9+1+4+1+9+5+7+1 = 37, 3 + 7 = 1

Money Number: 1

Once you have found your money number, you can get a sense for how you tend to relate to money. This can also be a number that you infuse into your money manifesting practices, such as by saving money in values that relate to your number. So, if your number was 1, saving $1, $10, $100, etc. would be ideal.

Here is a cheat sheet for how you likely relate to money based on your money number:

Money Number 1: You like to control your money and to be paid well for what you do.

Money Number 2: You make and spend money wisely.

Money Number 3: You have strong financial communication and negotiation skills.

Money Number 4: You prefer conservative career choices and work hard for money.

Money Number 5: You enjoy buying, selling, and making deals with people.

Money Number 6: Job stability and security is imperative for you.

Money Number 7: You enjoy making money through technical work.

Money Number 8: You will always be good at making money, no matter what.

Money Number 9: You make money to donate it, first and foremost.

Numbers for Motivation

Your motivation number is achieved by taking all of the vowels in your name (a, e, i, o, u) and adding their numerological value together to get your motivation number. Below is an example of how to find your motivation number using the name Sam Smith and a cheat sheet that will help you determine what your motivation number means.

Name: Sam Smith

Vowels: A I

Numerology: 1 + 9 = 10, 1 + 0 = 1

Motivation Number: 1

You can use the cheat sheet for the alphabet from Chapter 4 to help you determine what your motivation number is. Once you have found it, the numbers below will help guide you to discover what your number means about how you are motivated in life.

Motivation Number 1: You are motivated by independence, personal responsibility, and being inventive in life.

Motivation Number 2: You are motivated by working in groups, whether it is growing a family or teaming together with other people to launch a business idea.

Motivation Number 3: You are motivated by your need to communicate, to be around other people, and your desire to express yourself creatively.

Motivation Number 4: You are motivated by tradition, routine, and being a homebody.

Motivation Number 5: You are motivated by your craving for something new and different and you thrive in situations that do not revolve around routines and repetition.

Motivation Number 6: You are motivated by your family and your home life. You love taking care of your family and keeping everything in order on the home front.

Motivation Number 7: You are motivated by your constant curiosity and your need to learn more and know more. You love to ponder about the universe and life itself.

Motivation Number 8: You are motivated by large-scale projects, particularly those relating to leadership and management. The bigger the project, the more you are interested in it.

Motivation Number 9: You are motivated by your desire to benefit others and humanity as a whole, and you love being able to give back.

Numbers for Hidden Passions

We all have hidden talents and hidden passions, and numerology can help you find yours! Using the equation below, you can find your hidden passion number to discover what you may be interested in or good at that you do not yet know about! You can learn about your hidden passions by looking for numbers that repeat in your name. So, you want to take your name and find the numerical value of each letter and then pay close attention to any number that shows up multiple times. This number will say something about your hidden passions! Hint: you can have many!

We are going to use the sample name Kevin Clark to find out what a hidden talent chart should look like.

Name: Kevin Clark

Numerical Values: K = 2, E = 5, V = 6, I = 9, N = 5, C = 3, L = 3, A = 1, R = 2, K = 2.

Repeating Numbers: 2 (3 times,) 5 (2 times,) 3 (2 times.)

Hidden Passion Numbers: 2, 5, 3

Once you have found what numbers are repeating in your name, you can get a feel for what your hidden passion numbers are! Below is a cheat sheet of what each number represents in terms of what your hidden passions may be.

Hidden Passion Number 1: You are a warrior and a leader. You likely accelerate in competitive things such as politics or athletics.

Hidden Passion Number 2: You are highly sensitive and intuitive. You likely accelerate in things that require patience and persistence such as painting or building models.

Hidden Passion Number 3: You are a party animal! You likely accelerate in active and social events such as team sports, dancing, and comedy.

Hidden Passion Number 4: You are systematic and organized. You accelerate in reaching goals no matter how small or large, and no matter what field they lie in.

Hidden Passion Number 5: You are an adventurer and a traveler. You accelerate in adapting to change and are likely extremely good with words. You would do good with public relations work.

Hidden Passion Number 6: You are a dreamer and you love being of service. You accelerate in serving your community and your loved ones. You would make a great homemaker, partner or friend, or humanitarian.

Hidden Passion Number 7: You are highly intelligent and intuitive. You accelerate in activities relating to meditation and study and would make for a great spiritual leader or teacher.

Hidden Passion Number 8: You are extremely strong and successful. You accelerate in managing others, motivating others to do better, and identifying people's strengths and weaknesses.

Hidden Passion Number 9: You are a warm, compassionate, and generous individual. You accelerate in being a creative genius, although you may have hidden this talent deep within you at a young age. This seems to be common for hidden passion number 9 folks!

Numbers for Compatibility

If you are looking to see if you are a good fit with the person that you are considering entering a friendship or a romantic relationship with, you may be wondering what numbers you are most compatible with. Like astrological charts, numerology charts also have compatibility features and can be compared with your friend or partner's chart to get a feel for how compatible you are. When it comes to measuring compatibility, you will measure using your psychic number.

The following chart will tell you which numbers are most compatible.

	Most Compatible	Usually Compatible	Sort of Compatible	No
1	1, 5, 7	3, 9	8	2, 4
2	2, 4, 8	3, 6	9	1, 5
3	3, 6, 9	1, 2, 5		4, 7
4	2, 4, 8	6, 7		1, 3

5	1, 5, 7	3, 9	8	
6	3, 6, 9	2, 4, 8		1
7	1, 5, 7	4	9	
8	2, 4, 8	6	1, 5	
9	3, 6, 9	1, 5	2, 7	

Numbers for Balance

Your balance number will rarely influence you until you find that your life is off balance, and then it will begin to matter. When your life has gotten off balance, you can use this number to help you identify how you can get through emotional turmoil so that you can begin healing from the imbalance. You find your balance number by adding together the numerical value of your initials at birth. So, if your birth name was Toby David Smith, your initials would be T, D, S. Once you have found the numerical value of your initials, you have found the numerical value of your balance number.

Here is an example equation showing you how to achieve this number. You can refer to the alphabet chart in Chapter 4 to help you find your balance number.

Name at Birth: Toby David Smith

Initials: T, D, S

Numerical Value of Initials: T = 2, D = 4, S = 1

Equation: 2 + 4 + 1 = 7

Balance Number: 7

Once you have found your balance number, you can hold onto it and use it to guide you any time that you are experiencing an imbalance in your own life. Below you will find information on what each balance number means and how you can use it to guide you back to balance in your life.

> **Balance Number 1:** Continue to draw strength from yourself, but learn how to open up and receive support from your loved ones. When you need to find balance, learning how to step out of your natural independence and ask for help will be valuable.

> **Balance Number 2:** You are a very emotional number, so learning how to step away from intense emotional responses and into a more practical and logical response can be helpful. Critically consider your situation and choose the logical step forward. Your emotions will thank you.

> **Balance Number 3:** Avoid becoming overly emotional or trying to manipulate your way out of problems that you face. Instead, practice detaching from the problem and looking at it in a more objective way. This way, you can see the problem for what it truly is and find a reasonable solution to move forward.

> **Balance Number 4:** Be more lighthearted toward the issues that you are facing, and be sure to tap into your emotions. You may try to press through and force your way

forward, but this can only lead to more problems in most situations. Learning how to be more gentle and sensitive will be helpful.

Balance Number 5: You may find yourself frequently trying to avoid the problem that you are facing, which can lead to more problems. Learn how to ground your free spirit and tune into a logical way forward. Learning to stick through the pain can be helpful as it will lead you through your problems. They're often not as scary as you think.

Balance Number 6: You have a powerful ability to understand the problems that you are in and to see the problem from all angles. You can see the other perspectives easily, which helps you with discovering how you can find a harmonious solution. Just make sure that you also factor your own perspective into your problem-solving so you feel accounted for, too.

Balance Number 7: Attempting to retreat into yourself is not going to help you now. You may feel like isolating yourself, but this is not what you need. Spend time contemplating, but also be willing to face yourself and your emotions and then work with other people to solve your problems. Be calm and at ease with your emotional expression to avoid getting too overwhelmed by your emotional response.

Balance Number 8: Avoid trying to take control over everything and power your way through everything that comes your way. Instead, gently tap into your emotions and consult your feelings and inner needs. It is fine to take leadership and lead your way through, but be sure to do so with compassion and gentleness.

Balance Number 9: Look to others for advice and have empathy for their situations. You relate well to other people to empathize with people who have been through what you are going through is a great opportunity to "feel" into the right solution for you. This is going to help you see the bigger picture so that you can find success in your problem-solving.

CHAPTER 17
Numerology, Astrology, And Tarot

Numerology, astrology, and tarot all connect together. Each of these divinity reading styles have their own unique way that they fit together with the other two, yet they all come together to develop a powerful reading format for all. If you have ever been drawn to astrology or tarot, chances are you will be surprised to learn that numerology is not too different from these two reading styles. Read on to learn more about how they all connect together!

Numerology's Connection to Astrology
Astrology is the study of the movement between the stars and the planet, and the belief is that the planets have different meanings for people based on where they are stationed. In astrology, there are twelve houses, or stations where their chart will "stop in." These houses are each ruled by a specific planet, and the planet's meaning often correlates with the meaning of the number of the house itself.

Below is a cheat sheet of the 12 different houses and their astrological and numerological meanings.

> **House 1:** Ruled by Aries, the independent and strong leader of the zodiac. Number 1 also relates to independence, strength, and leadership.

House 2: Ruled by Taurus, the steady, fixed, and focused sign that does not like change. Number 2 also likes to be detail oriented and dislikes sudden changes.

House 3: Ruled by Gemini, a sociable, skilled, and quick-witted sign. Number 3 is also associated with being sociable, skilled, and quick-witted.

House 4: Ruled by Cancer, a sensitive, nurturing sign that is known for having constant mood swings. Number 4 is known for being dependable and calm, although reactive meaning that their moods can shift rather rapidly.

House 5: Ruled by Leo, this sign is proud, egotistical, and sometimes dramatic. They also crave freedom. Number 5 is also a freedom-loving number that can be proud, egotistical, and sometimes dramatic.

House 6: Ruled by Virgo, this sign is detail-oriented, worrisome, and very picky. They like things to be a specific way, which is also relevant for number 6.

House 7: Ruled by Libra, this sign is very introspective, likes balance and justice, and can be indecisive. Number 7 is also known for being very introspective and wise, and they crave balance.

House 8: Ruled by Scorpio, this sign can be very controlling, passionate, and even revengeful. They like to have power. Number 8 is also very controlling and likes to have the power, and finds themselves very passionate sometimes to the point of being revengeful.

House 9: Ruled by Sagittarius, this sign can be philosophical, careless, and free-spirited. Number 9s are also this way, and can be very inspired by others.

House 10: Ruled by Capricorn, this sign is very realistic and often cold in their approach. They like public status and career. Number 10 breaks down to number one is often very cold and realistic in their leadership style, and also crave popularity.

House 11: Ruled by Aquarius, this sign is a humanitarian, outgoing, and often aloof. This resonates with master number 11 energy which is also very invested in these qualities, sometimes even being considered an Earth Angel.

House 12: Ruled by Pisces, this sign is emotional, has their head in the clouds, and is very romantic and shy. Number 12 is also known for being suspended between the physical and spiritual worlds and can be very emotional and overly sensitive.

Numerology's Connection to Tarot

Numerology also has a strong connection to tarot, as each tarot card in a standard 78 card deck is associated with a number. In tarot, the cards are read based on what number they are in a suit, as this number contributes to the meaning. For example, a card with a number one on it will represent a new beginning in that particular area of life.

Below is a great cheat sheet of how the numbers relate to tarot readings:

Number 1: Signifies new beginnings and the first step on a journey. This is often considered the purest element of each suit in the tarot and generally appears when someone is about to start something new in their life.

Number 2: This is the number of partnership and will often reflect the choices that a person is going to make in their life. The number two card in any suit will often show up at a time of consideration or introspection, and will help a person decide on what path they need to be taking in their life.

Number 3: In Tarot, the number three reflects natural progression and the growth of a situation. This is where an idea turns into an actual new process, powered by all of that number three energy. This is the number of socialness and team building.

Number 4: Four represents foundations in the tarot. In this number, we are vibrating at the energy of practicality and structured thinking. This card will appear when a certain level of success has been obtained and the individual is ready to begin growing on that success.

Number 5: Instability and change can enter a person's life if a card with the number five shows up in their reading. True to the freedom seeking adventurous qualities of a number five's energy, any fives in a tarot deck often reflect this instability, too.

Number 6: When you bring out a number six card, you are stepping into relief from the flightiness of number five energy. Oftentimes community will be shown in the number six card and it will encourage people to reach out to people in their support network in one way or another.

Number 7: When the seven arrives in a tarot reading, you are being asked to have faith and be patient in your journey. At this point you are likely going to go through a period of self-awareness and reflection so that you can get through whatever growth phase you are currently working on.

Number 8: In the tarot deck, number eight reflects progress. When a number eight card shows up you can feel confident that you have been developing a high level of success in some area of your life. You are currently managing things well there, and you are being congratulated for a job well done.

Number 9: In tarot number nine reflects the completion of a cycle, just as it would in numerology. Even though the tarot deck goes to number 10, number 9 is where we start to see this completion cycle come through.

Number 10: This is the final card in the sequence and when it comes to the connection between numerology and tarot, this card refers to the exact moment before we transition from completion to a new beginning once again. This is the moment before a rebirth in life.

CHAPTER 18
9-Year Cycles

Numerology sees everything as a cycle. A cycle of 9, to be exact. From the single digit of number 1 to the single digit of number 9, everything is believed to be a cycle in numerology. This means that you complete another cycle when you are 9, 18, 27, 36, 45, 54, 63, 72, 81, 90, and 99 years old. Knowing where you lie in a 9-year cycle can help you determine where you are at in your life and what you are presently working on creating or manifesting.

Below you will find what you can expect in each yearly cycle.

Year 1 Cycle
Your year one cycle can be linked to new beginnings and fresh starts. This is where you start planting seeds for what you are going to be learning about and growing with over the next nine years. Here, pay close attention to what you are setting into motion as it will guide you through your lessons in the years to come.

Year 2 Cycle
Year two is a year for gradual progress. You do not want to rush too quickly, so avoid putting too much pressure on yourself to get everything done or to move on to the next step. Instead, focus on building out your network and connecting with people who are going to be able to support you in the coming years. Nurture these connections.

Year 3 Cycle

In a three year you want to focus on cultivating happiness. In your two year you may have focused more on others as you nurture your relationships for your own future growth. This year, focus on bringing in your own happiness and serving yourself a little more. Here, you get to develop even further and set your growth in real motion.

Year 4 Cycle

A four year is about making breakthroughs and big changes. In your fourth year of any cycle you are going to find yourself seeing your work bringing plenty of new successes to fruition. While you can tell that you have not reached fruition yet, you will receive many opportunities to affirm your growth and progress in this year.

Year 5 Cycle

Year five is going to bring you more new experiences, particularly those that are relevant to your growth. In a year five cycle you will have plenty of opportunities to learn through adventure, journey, and change. You are also going to learn from your mistakes as this will be a very hands-on year for you to embrace your growth.

Year 6 Cycle

The six year is where you get to reinvent yourself after a year of growth and change. Here is where you are going to start really looking deeper into your journey and deciding on what feels right for you and what it is that you want to create in your life. You are going to be cultivating your relationships, balancing, healing, and loving more.

Year 7 Cycle
A year seven in your cycles is the year of inner adventure and growth. Here you are going to be looking inward at all of your growth and finding opportunities to embrace and embody it. Any lesson you have been working through over the past seven years will start to look different to you as you begin fully understanding what they all mean, often retroactively.

Year 8 Cycle
A year eight cycle is about developing your personal power and self-confidence. This year you are journeying deeper into a state of self-awareness and self-development. You are starting to reap the rewards of your lessons as you are beginning to feel far more confident in what you know, and in applying what you know to your life. You will achieve a lot this year.

Year 9 Cycle
In year nine you are going to find yourself going through a lot of reflection. During this part of the nine-year cycle you will be looking back to see what you have learned and what you have gained. Consider this to be a consolidation period in your life where

you come to realize what everything meant, how you have grown from it, and what you can officially release from your life.

CHAPTER 19
Numerology And Reincarnation

In addition to having meanings pertaining to each year, the nine different cycles are also said to have meanings pertaining to each incarnation. In numerology, it is believed that you will reincarnate nine times with each incarnation being guided by lessons associated with the number of incarnations you have had. In this chapter you will discover what each incarnation is said to mean. You can discover what incarnation you are on based on what your destiny number is on your numerology chart.

First Incarnation
Your first incarnation on Earth is said to be very innocent, as you are in your first life cycle. For this life cycle you are very young in your spiritual maturity and you have not had much opportunity to develop an understanding of Earth itself. This first incarnation does not mean that your soul is young, but it does mean that your soul is new to Earth.

Second Incarnation
Your second incarnation is about connection and stability. In this lifetime you will likely connect with your soul family, or souls who incarnated with the sole purpose of meeting you here on Earth to work through karmic lessons together. You will spend this lifetime

learning how to respect and appreciate the connection of others as you grow away from the fierce independence of your first life cycle.

Third Incarnation

In your third life cycle your soul is starting to remember what life is all about, so you are likely going to be more outgoing and engaged in Earthly things. This will have a very immature or self-centered approach as you have not yet learned how to experience all of life with other people. While other people will definitely be around, you will be prone to seeing them as a part of your experience, rather than all of you as being a part of the collective experience.

Fourth Incarnation

Your fourth incarnation will be about doing soul work. Here is where you will be starting to mature more, and with that maturity might come some pessimism or pain. You are starting to realize the reality of nonduality, or of being an independent in a highly connected collective. You will be doing a lot of soul work, so to speak.

Fifth Incarnation

Your fifth incarnation will be a huge swing away from the serious and focused fourth incarnation as you start enjoying freedom and adventure. You will spend this lifetime denying what comes naturally to you in order to discover new things about the world around you. You want to see, learn, and experience as much as you possibly can in this life cycle.

Sixth Incarnation

Your sixth incarnation is a period where you are going to start settling down. After an incarnation of adventure and freedom, your soul will be looking to gain the experience of settling down and embracing commitment. You will be learning how to commit to living as a part of a community or a group effectively.

Seventh Incarnation

Your seventh incarnation will be about growth and learning, so you will likely spend most of this life cycle engaging in some form of study. After everything you have learned in the past six life cycles you are ready to start putting it all together, and so you are doing this through the introspective and curious seventh incarnation.

Eighth Incarnation

In your eighth incarnation you are growing on your wisdom gained in the seventh incarnation so that you can begin embodying the true strength of your soul. You will likely want to micromanage the integration of your new information into your present life cycle so that you can be positive that it will be experienced on one level or another.

Ninth Incarnation

In your ninth incarnation you are believed to be in your final life cycle, and with this cycle you are going to have your true embodiment experience. You have experienced many dualities and lessons in the past nine life cycles and now you are embodying them on a soul level with deep soulful maturity. You are *being* you in this life cycle, and it shows.

CONCLUSION

Congratulations on completing *Numerology for Beginners!*

This book was written to help you explore the vast world of numerology and begin to understand just what this divinity tool has to offer. Numerology has been used for years, and it is a highly valuable tool that can help you discover more about yourself and how you can navigate your life in alignment with who you truly are. By tapping into your numbers and learning how to read your chart you can explore the vast world of you through a totally new perspective!

I hope that this book has supported you in understanding what numerology is, why it is so important, how it works, and what you can do to apply it to your life. Applying numerology to your life by learning how to create and read your own chart can be powerful. I hope that you were able to learn more about yourself, resonate with your numbers, and feel a greater sense of self-awareness and personal understanding through this book.

The next step after reading this book is recognizing that numerology is a powerful tool that you can always continue learning about. If you want to go beyond reading your own chart and really getting deeper into the different numbers and how they can be read in other ways, I encourage you to continue studying numerology. You will likely be surprised to find out that there is so much to learn! You can also start connecting your numerology practice to your astrology or tarot practice, or even using numerology to lead you into a healthy astrology or tarot practice to help you discover even more about yourself.

The more that you invest in understanding yourself through crafts like numerology, the easier it is for you to develop yourself along this journey. It is important to understand that tools like numerology are only meant to be used as a guide and not as a strict rule book in your life. As you read through your chart and reflect on it, remember that you may find areas where you do not resonate with your chart simply because you are a unique individual. Notice where you do resonate, and do not be afraid to overlook the areas where you do not resonate. You may find that you can find an even deeper resonance by going back to the double-digit number before the single digit number to help you resonate even deeper. In other numbers, you may completely identify with the primary number and find that it tells you plenty. To summarize, there is so much to be learned about yourself through numerology, but the ultimate learning comes from reflecting on it and seeing how it actually relates to you in your lifetime. This way, you can learn not only about numerology, but about yourself, too.

It is a good idea to write your chart down on paper or in a document so that you can reflect back on it whenever you need to. Many people find that their charts become valuable to them at many points in life, and they reference back to it frequently. As a result, they are able to get great information about how they can move through different phases of their life, what they can expect from the people around them, and how they make better decisions.

Regularly reflecting back on your chart can be a valuable opportunity for you to move in alignment with your true soul, which is the biggest benefit of numerology.

At the end of the day, the more you can come into alignment with yourself through tools like numerology, the more balanced your life is going to become. The key here is to understand your tendencies and patterns and realize that being empowered with this information means that you can start making more informed decisions. Numerology is not about being locked into a specific pattern or "doomed" to a certain lifestyle, but instead it is about learning how to live in flow with yourself in this lifetime.

Lastly, if you enjoyed this book, I ask that you please take the time to honestly review it on Amazon. Your feedback would be greatly appreciated.

Thank you, and enjoy!

Book Description

Numerology is a form of fortune telling that dates all the way back to the late 500 B.C times. Believed to be founded by Greek philosopher Pythagoras, this divinity reading style has been widely shared amongst the mystical community for years. In this handy guide those who are interested in learning about numerology can learn everything they need to know to get started.

This book is an excellent learning guide for those who are brand new to fortune telling altogether, or for those who have already engaged in other practices like astrology or tarot and who are ready to expand their understanding. Despite being written for beginners, this book goes deep into great information about numerology so that you can feel confident in your understanding by the time you are done!

If you are ready to learn about numerology and start discovering more about yourself and your loved ones through this divinity practice, grab your copy of *Numerology for Beginners* today and get started!

In This Book You Will Learn About...

- What numerology is, how it works, and how you can read numbers
- Where numerology comes from and how it developed
- How modern numerology differs from historical numerology

- The different numbers in your chart and how you can calculate them
- What each number in your chart says about who you are
- The energies associated with each different number
- Specific information about the different numbers based on their placements
- How to find your more advanced numbers, such as your money number or your hidden talent number
- How yearly cycles are influenced by the numbers
- What each yearly cycle means and what you will learn
- Reincarnation and numerology
- What your present incarnation means for your destiny
- And more!

CPSIA information can be obtained
at www.ICGtesting.com
Printed in the USA
BVHW041356120521
607043BV00003B/704